ROCK ART OF THE AMERICAN INDIAN

ROCK

AMERICAN

Written and illustrated by

CAMPBELL GRANT

THOMAS Y. CROWELL COMPANY

New York, Established 1834

ART OF THE
NDIAN

For Lou, Gordon, Roxanne, Sheila, and Douglas

1   2   3   4   5   6   7   8   9   10

FOREWORD

With the proliferation of writings on primitive art, it is remarkable to note that this book by Campbell Grant is the first general study of rock art in North America. While rock art has always occupied a paramount position in studies of European and African prehistory, it has been almost totally absent from similar studies of North America. In fact, even recent general histories of primitive or prehistoric art convey the impression that the only significant contribution of this continent lies in the sculpture of the Northwest Coast and the pottery of the Southwest. Campbell Grant has done much to dispel this limited view. His numerous articles and above all his recent book, *The Rock Paintings of the Chumash,* are notable contributions to the study of primitive art.

The author combines in his approach to his subject the seriousness and objectivity of the anthropologist with the sensitivity and perceptiveness of the artist. This present study well illustrates the advantages to be gained by looking at primitive art from the points of view of both the art historian and the anthropologist. This is especially apparent in any attempt to discern broad stylistic patterns in time and space. It is the formal aspects of an art form, not its subject matter or technique, that make it possible to distinguish one style from another. The different stylistic modes of rendering an individual form basically establish and distinguish one style from another.

One myth dispelled by this study of North American rock art is that the primitive artist approaches his work with a high regard for the nature of his medium and for the surface upon which it is placed. In every instance in North America where a single style is represented in both painted and engraved examples, the artist's major concern has been to render the form in as identical a fashion as possible, and to minimize or

v

to gloss over differences in technique. Thus technique was a means for the artist to realize subject matter through form; it did not form an essential element of the expressive language of the painting or engraving.

Another theoretical problem that the author has touched upon is the fundamental question of the place of art-as-art in prehistoric societies. The argument that "art for art's sake" did not exist within prehistoric societies is in reality meaningless. From ethnological studies of primitive cultures, it is obvious that all groups shared a basic aesthetic sensibility. A vast majority (perhaps all) of the material objects manufactured by man contain an aesthetic element to one degree or another. This is especially true in primitive cultures. In some instances the aesthetic element appears as a conscious addition, something added to the primary function of the object; in other cases it is so completely interwoven that the primary function and the aesthetic element are essentially one.

The question to be asked then is not whether "art for art's sake" existed in primitive society, but rather what form the art assumed and what the function of art was within a given society. Using the term religious in its broadest sense, there can be little doubt, as Campbell Grant points out, that the prime function of most North American rock art was ritualistic. At the same time, though, one should not overlook the fact that through its use of a visual form, each painting or engraving also acquired an aesthetic content. Thus one can readily see how closely interwoven are the inquiries of the anthropologist and the art historian into primitive art. If one is to look into the function of art in a primitive or prehistoric society, as the anthropologist does, he must first understand the basic nature of man's aesthetic sensibility, and then he must understand the form, i.e., the style, through which this sensibility has been expressed. It is the task of the art historian to provide an understanding of this aesthetic sensibility and of how it has been realized in form.

It also is hoped that this book will provoke other anthropologists and art historians to devote more serious study to this neglected aspect of North American primitive art. As Campbell Grant has indicated, there are really few areas in North America that have been thoroughly recorded, let alone thoroughly studied. Nor have there been any penetrating studies of the movements and extreme intermixing of styles that occurred in North America. There is as well the fascinating subject of sources, especially the diffusion of many basic elements northward from Mexico.

This study by Campbell Grant of the rock art of North America is then an excellent and perceptive example of how the disciplines of anthropology and art history may be combined to produce a meaningful picture of an extremely significant aspect of man's prehistoric past.

DAVID GEBHARD

University of California, Santa Barbara

PREFACE

In 1960, I saw my first rock painting in the rugged San Rafael Mountains near Santa Barbara, California. With the support of the Santa Barbara Museum of Natural History, I undertook the job of recording all such sites in the region. In three years of intensive field work, the number of known rock-art sites was raised from 17 to over 80. Later the study was expanded to include all of California and some adjoining states. This work was supported by grants from the National Science Foundation and resulted in a number of articles on the subject.

In the fall of 1964, I was asked by the editors of Thomas Y. Crowell Company if I would consider doing a book on the rock art of North America. My immediate reaction was to turn down the idea. The information necessary to put together such a project was simply not available. However, with considerable misgivings, I agreed to explore the literature and to see if it would be possible to obtain the many photographs that would be required. My two prime needs were information on site locations and picture material. Hundreds of letters were sent off to universities, museums, historical and archaeological societies, national parks and monuments, and many individuals, some of whom had written articles and others of whom had collections of photographs. The response was overwhelming. Armed with the information I received, I took a 12,000-mile trek through the country visiting sites, photographing and taking notes. But even such a trip was not nearly enough to cover the subject. I still had to depend in great part on the firsthand information and photographs of others who had done work in the field.

Before I was through, I had become deeply indebted to a great many people. Without their help, this book would not have been possible.

I am very grateful to the following people who took the time to answer my questions, lend books, give articles and reprints, and supply me with the all-important photographs: Donald N. Abbott, C. Melvin Aikens, Robert Babcock, Eric Barney, Roland E. Beschel, Clark W. Brott, William J. Buckles, H. Thomas Cain, Carl H. Chapman, David L. Cole, Carl Compton, Stuart W. Conner, Harold Cundy, Joseph Doctor, Frank Fryman, Jr., Robert E. Greengo, Gutorm Gjessing, Henry Hadlock, Roderick Haig-Brown, W. N. Irving, Frank M. Jones, Tim Jones, Frederica de Laguna, Sherman P. Lawton, Douglas Leechman, R. S. MacNeish, Charles R. McGimsey, Carling Malouf, Irving M. Peithman, William J. Schaldach, Carl Schuster, Agnes Sims, Ivar Skarland, James L. Swauger, Raymond H. Thompson, Spencer A. Waters, Henry Weldon, Joe Ben Wheat, Warren Wittry, and H. M. Wormington.

In addition, I am indebted to the following people who furnished photographic material: Mrs. Heber Bennion, Jr., Dean R. Brimhall, Carl Browall, Joan Colbrook, Katherine Capes, Harold S. Colton, John E. Cook, Dorothy Dancker, Edward B. Danson, Alfred E. Dittert, Jr., Henry During, Erle Stanley Gardner, James C. Garner, Jeanne B. Hillis, Howard Hughes, Carl E. Jepsen, Merritt S. Johnston, Thomas F. Kehoe, Edward L. Keithahn, Olive Kelsall, Kenneth E. Kidd, Monroe P. Killy, Paul W. Klammer, Clement W. Meighan, Franklin V. Montford, Thomas Mulhern, Dorris L. Olds, Choral Pepper, Jean M. Pinkley, Velma Pontoni, Annie Sanders, Polly Schaafsma, Earl M. Semingsen, James Sleznick, Jr., Dean Snow, Christy G. Turner, Ronald Wauer, Merle W. Wells, Harry Wills, and Thomas A. Witty.

I am especially grateful to Frank Magre for making available his unpublished work on the rock drawings of Missouri; to Selwyn Dewdney, whose Canadian studies made the Northern Woodland section possible; and to Robert F. Heizer of the University of California, who has patiently answered endless questions over a period of years. John J. Cawley, Donald Martin, and Dale Ritter were especially helpful in furnishing me with site records and many fine photographs. Throughout the project, I was aided by the National Park Service, the U.S. Geological Survey, and the National Museum of Canada.

I am particularly indebted to the late Dr. Donald Scott of the Peabody Museum and David Gebhard of the University of California, Santa Barbara, leading authorities on prehistoric rock drawings, for their reading and checking the manuscript and for their many suggestions.

Finally, I am very much obliged to Barbara Lawrence, who typed and checked the various drafts of the manuscript from my almost illegible originals.

All text drawings and photographs without credit lines are by the author.

CONTENTS

COLOR PLATES (following page 114)

PHOTOGRAPHS AND DRAWINGS

MAPS

Part I

THE ARTISTS AND THEIR ART

1 BACKGROUND

In the summer of 1879, Marcelino de Sautuola, an amateur archaeologist, was excavating at the entrance to the cave of Altamira in northern Spain. His five-year-old daughter, playing inside, looked up at the roof of the cavern and discovered the now celebrated paintings of bison made during the last ice age by Paleolithic cave-dwelling hunters.

This discovery led to many others in southern France and northern Spain and the study of rock drawings began. The paintings and engravings were almost invariably of long-extinct animals like the mammoth and woolly rhinoceros, and the earliest may be nearly 30,000 years old.

The published descriptions of these finds by the pioneer investigator Henri Breuil created a worldwide interest in the subject of rock art and spectacular new discoveries have been made in many lands—the great Tassili complex of drawings in the Sahara Desert, the beautiful animal paintings in central and south Africa, and the weird *wondjina* and X-ray pictures from Australia. All these have been described in handsomely illustrated books.

It is curious that North American rock art is practically unknown to the general reading public. The existence of innumerable rock drawings in the western states was often noted in the writings of the early explorers and actually many articles and a few books have been written on the subject. Unfortunately, however, most of these are buried in obscure scientific publications, available only to the researcher, or are in local newspaper articles or back issues of a few magazines, particularly *Arizona Highways* and *Desert Magazine*.

This book is an attempt to synthesize present knowledge on the subject. The study has entailed a thorough search of the literature, many personal communications with investigators, and considerable field work.

Red, white, and black painting, Caliente Range, California.

3

Unfortunately a single volume on such a complex subject can serve only as an introduction to a much neglected part of our country's heritage.

Many of the points covered in this book, particularly those dealing with age and interpretation, are debatable and as new evidence is turned up, present views will change to fit such evidence.

Scattered through the rocky section of North America are great numbers of curious paintings and carvings. Many of the pictures are done with great care and skill—others are mere scrawls. In some regions the drawings are highly abstract while in others the dominant style is realistic. The working surface is usually granite, sandstone, or basalt, though rock art has been found on almost every kind of stone in the country.

The existence of rock art in North America was noticed by many of the early explorers. Father Jacques Marquette, exploring down the Mississippi in 1673, described several painted monsters on a cliff near the present site of Alton, Illinois. Dighton Rock in Massachusetts, covered with strange designs, has been studied and argued over since the first drawings were made of it in 1680. Father Eusebio Kino described and mapped the "Painted Rocks" (actually engravings) near Gila Bend, Arizona, in 1711, and in 1776 the explorer Father Silvestre de Escalante, attempting to find a land route from Mexico to Monterey, saw carved rock figures in western Colorado. As settlers traveled through the mountains of the Southwest in the early nineteenth century, great numbers of drawings on rocks were noted.

The first serious scientific study of American rock art was made by Colonel Garrick Mallery in 1886. This "preliminary paper," *Pictographs of the North American Indians*, ran to 256 pages and discussed picture making by Indians on all sorts of materials—stone, wood, bone, and skin. Seven years later Mallery produced his magnum opus, the monumental *Picture Writing of the American Indian*—822 pages of scholarly research, of which about a quarter was devoted to rock art.

This formidable volume, issued by the Bureau of American Ethnology, became (and still is) the foremost authority on the subject and until the present no further attempt has been made at a broad study. There has been a great deal of work on specific sites and regional complexes but such work, with some notable exceptions, has been confined to scientific literature. A few leading archaeologists, like Robert F. Heizer and Clement Meighan of the University of California, have been actively attacking the subject for a number of years, and *Prehistoric Rock Art of Nevada and Eastern California*, by Robert Heizer and Martin Baumhoff, published in 1962, is a major work on the rock pictures.

Many professional archaeologists in the United States, however, have been avoiding the problems raised by rock-art sites because of the difficulty of correlating the rock art with specific native cultures. Since there has always been more than enough digging to be done at important sites, the consideration of the rock drawings has been continually shelved for the future. The reluctance of professionals to enter the field has brought workers into the vacuum from amateur groups, and valuable local site surveys have been published by many state and county archaeological societies.

Since the publication of Mallery's great work, many thousands of sites have been recorded west of the Mississippi; the number east of the Mississippi has grown little since his time. The recording of sites in Canada has hardly begun, and here again the field work is being conducted by tireless amateurs like Selwyn Dewdney, an artist from Ontario. In Mexico, where investigation of the superb high civilizations has beguiled the time and energies of professionals for generations, the humble rock pictures have been almost completely neglected. Although there must be many thousands of sites in northern Mexico (treated in the present work as part of the Southwest), there are only about a dozen slim articles on the subject.

It is not surprising that most of the rock pictures are found in the West. From the Rocky Mountains to the Pacific, the land mass is folded into innumerable rocky ranges cut by great river systems. Smooth stone surfaces for the artist's brush or stone chisel are to be found almost everywhere. This is the region through which passed the major continental migrations moving down into Mexico and South America and peoples of many culture patterns have been living in this land of rocks for many thousands of years.

The question that comes up most frequently is, Who made these strange and mysterious drawings on stone? Unhappily the long silence on the subject by the archaeologists has brought hordes of eager amateurs into the picture with endless fanciful explanations. All sorts of full-fledged Old World people are seen wandering about and leaving messages on stone—Greeks, Chinese, Romans, Egyptians. Even the long-suffering Lost Tribes of Israel are dragged in. "Lost Continents" such as Mu and Atlantis are related to rock pictures—books and articles are written in defense of the most absurd theories. Some enthusiasts spend their time trying to decipher the "writings," believing that somewhere a key exists that will unlock fabulous secrets usually connected with lost treasures. Many rock drawings are seen as maps to such sites; others are Masonic symbols or zodiac signs. There is almost no pseudoscientific nonsense that has not at some time been staunchly upheld by the incurably imaginative "researchers."

These people all have one thing in common—they conduct their investigations in reverse. They have a pet theory and then look for evidence

Pecked drawing from Black Canyon, southeastern California. From photograph by John Cawley.

to support it, discarding anything that seems to disprove the cherished idea. One such person who had spent many years in pursuit of rock drawings and their meaning recently wrote that he had never read any books on the subject as this would have interfered with his research! These amateur experts are loath to accept a simple explanation. The idea that an ordinary Indian would spend considerable time pecking out an intricate design in hard stone to help insure his wife's bearing him a healthy man-child is too humdrum. No consideration is given by these people to the fact that the American Indian did not think as we are trained to and he did not interpret his ideas as we do. His world was largely a world of the supernatural and he often pictured unseen beings and forces on stone.

The rock pictures in North America were the creations of the American Indian and no one else. As any understanding of American rock art must be based on some knowledge of its creators, it will be well to start at the beginning.

The North America of 20,000 years ago was a hunter's paradise. The familiar big-game animals, such as moose, caribou, mountain sheep, buffalo, musk-ox, and elk, were here in countless numbers and with them were many animals now extinct, such as the giant ground sloth, the woolly mammoth, the mastodon, a giant buffalo, the horse, and the camel. The only thing missing was the hunter. Man had not appeared in the New World.

The Pleistocene or Ice Age was drawing to a close but the Wisconsin ice sheet still covered most of the northern half of the continent, extending as far south as central Iowa. About 15,000 years ago, the ice sheet began its final retreat, opening up an ice-free route through the MacKenzie River valley. The great masses of water withdrawn from the oceans to build the glaciers had lowered the sea level several hundreds of feet and where Alaska and Siberia nearly meet at the Bering Strait, a broad land bridge connected the continents. The stage was set in North America to receive visitors. Let us see what was happening in Siberia.

The greater part of Siberia remained unglaciated during the Wisconsin and here we must look for the first people to enter the New World. Doubtless they were small bands of hunters, following the big game as it moved seeking forage. Some time before 10,000 B.C., some such group of fur-clad hunters went farther east than ever before and so began the population of North America. The American "Indian" had arrived.

The earliest archaeological finds of man in the New World show definite Australoid characteristics—low brow ridges, protruding jaws, and long, narrow head—certainly a far cry from the hawk-nosed Mongoloid of the Western Plains. Down through the centuries, small groups of hunters straggled over from Siberia and many diverse strains have been

Black and red painting, Concho County, Texas. Redrawn from A. T. Jackson.

Scratched drawings of moose, Kedgemakooge Lake, Nova Scotia. Redrawn from Garrick Mallery, 1893.

identified. Harold Gladwin, in *Men Out of Asia*, identifies five migrations —Australoid, Negroid, Algonquian, Eskimo, and finally Mongoloid, the type that was to blend with and dominate all others. Though other writers are far less explicit than Gladwin, it is certain that the present-day Indian is a composite, ranging from tall and thin to short and stout, with a skin coloring from dark brown to nearly white. But, from the Arctic Ocean to Tierra del Fuego, Indians all share one dominant Mongoloid characteristic—straight black hair.

There were several routes open to the first migrants. Most of Alaska, surprisingly, was unglaciated and the hunting parties could have followed the game up the Yukon River to the MacKenzie drainage then south to the Western Plains. Another possibility was to follow the Alaskan coast-line north, travel east along the Brooks Range to the mouth of the Mac-Kenzie, then south to the plains. A third route would skirt the ice shelf along the Pacific coast (human remains on Santa Rosa Island off the southern California coast have been dated at over 10,000 years old).

The country seen by the first arrivals south of the ice sheets was profoundly different from what we know today. During the latter half of the Wisconsin glaciation, a period of heavy and widespread rains known as the "Great Pluvial" created many huge lakes, particularly in the Great Basin. Only a tiny fraction of ancient Lake Bonneville, at one time the size of Lake Superior, remains—the Great Salt Lake. Forests and immense grasslands covered the Southwest, creating conditions for big game similar to those still found in central Africa.

As the glaciers continued their retreat, the oceans rose and the land bridge connecting the continents was covered by water. But the crossing was still possible by boat or on foot when the winter ice formed, and the migrations continued. Driven by pressure from people to the south or following game, the hunters continued to move into the New World. The major movement was along the slopes of the Rockies, fanning out to east and west, or south along the Sierra Madre Mountains in Mexico,

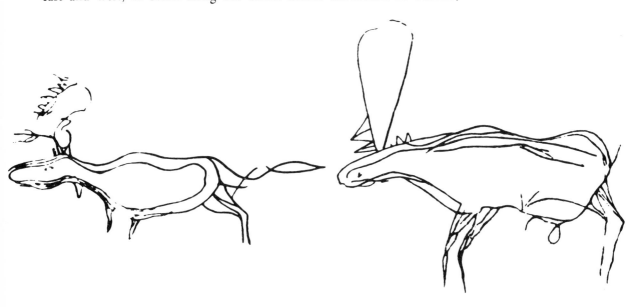

through Central America into South America and finally to Tierra del Fuego.

The first hunters of whom we have definite knowledge made excellent tools and projectile points. Their chief weapon was the spear, hand thrown or cast with a spear thrower or *atlatl*—the bow was a much later introduction. With this puny arsenal, early man hunted and in his camp refuse we find the bones of many extinct animals. Through the radio-carbon-dating method, we know roughly when some of these animals died out. Most—including the native horse and camel—disappeared between 10,000 and 8,000 years ago, with a terminal date of around 6,000 years ago for the mastodon.[1] What caused this great extinction is unknown but changing climate and hunting pressure from man must have played a large part. As the climate in the Southwest grew drier, and the game scarcer, many hunting groups were reduced to deer, mountain sheep, and rabbits. Their diet was augmented by edible seeds and roots and a food-gathering culture began. There is a milling stone from this period dated about 5400 B.C.

According to a recent article by Dr. Richard S. MacNeish, an astonishing thing was taking place about 5000 B.C. in the Valley of Tehuacan, in south-central Mexico—the people had discovered agriculture.[2] Cave remains show that several varieties of beans, chili, squashes, and, most important, corn, had been domesticated. Similar remains of corn have been found in Bat Cave, Arizona, and radiocarbon dating indicated they were between 4,000 and 5,000 years old. With this development village life was first established and it became prevalent throughout most of the Southwest at an early period.

At least four thousand years ago a new group of people began to move into the New World. Eventually these Indians occupied the forested country from Puget Sound to Newfoundland, all sharing a common Algonquian-language stock.[3] Cord-marked pottery, the bow, and the domesticated dog were introduced sometime during this period. These newcomers were hunters, creating a Woodland culture in Canada and the northern United States. Later they augmented this with agriculture in the areas where climate permitted. The country was filling up and groups of people were moving around or being pushed out by stronger groups seeking greener pastures. The Eskimo arrived fully equipped to face life along the bleak Arctic coasts and here they remain today. Other people settled in the Northwest and may have come by sea. They shared some rather extraordinary things with the Maoris of New Zealand—huge sailing canoes, plank houses with gable ends, and feather mantles.[4]

Uto-Aztecan-speaking nomads moved into the Great Basin, the Southwest, and on into Mexico. Prominent in this group were the Shoshone, Paiute, Hopi, Tanoan Pueblo, and Comanche in the United States and the

Red Eskimo painting,
Cook Inlet, Alaska.
Redrawn from
Frederica de
Laguna, 1933.

Aztec in Mexico. Tribes sharing the Athabascan language pushed down into northwestern Canada where they are still found. By A.D. 900 two vigorous tribes from this area, the Navajo and Apache, had left the main group and were moving down into the Southwest.

A brief look at the known prehistory of the Southwest is important as this area is one of the major rock-art regions in North America. Through intensive study of the ruins, many of which have been dated by tree-ring counts from building timbers, and identification of cultures through pottery association, building techniques, and artifacts, we know a good deal about the Southwest from about the birth of Christ to the coming of the whites.

At about A.D. 200 small groups of hunters and foragers, and primitive agriculturists raising corn, squash, and cotton, were living in cave shelters from southern Nevada to western Texas. The term Anasazi (Navajo for "the old ones") is usually applied to the people living in the "Four Corners" area, where Utah, Arizona, New Mexico, and Colorado meet. Their early phase, called Basketmaker, later evolved into the Pueblo culture. People with much the same Basketmaker culture were living in the upper Gila drainage and as far east as western Texas. All made baskets but true pottery had not yet appeared. Not long after A.D. 200 new ideas were gradually introduced, possibly by people moving in from the plains to the east. They brought the bow and arrow, pottery, and the rectangular earth lodge.

By A.D. 600 the Anasazi had occupied more territory but were still confined to the general area of the Four Corners. The foragers of southeastern Arizona were in contact with people from Mexico who brought, among other things, beans, a new type of corn, and polished pottery. The movement of people and the assimilation of new ideas continued for many years. By 700 the Hohokam migration from Mexico had introduced a relatively high culture to the Southwest. These people had advanced ideas on canal irrigation, built large ball courts, made excellent decorated pottery, and carved skillfully in stone. By 900 people still lived in small one-family houses and the communal multistoried pueblo had not yet appeared. Various peoples like the Mimbres, Mesa Verde, and Hohokam continued to develop their distinctive cultures. The life was a peaceful agricultural one but pressure was beginning to come from the outside, forcing some of the peripheral settlements to be abandoned. Nomadic Athabascan tribes—the restless, aggressive Navajos and Apaches—were moving down along the Rockies from western Canada.

As the pressure increased, scattered groups began to concentrate toward the north in refuge areas where the first fortresslike pueblos were built, culminating in such great structures as Pueblo Bonito. About 1100, as the Athabascan invasion grew, the southwestern tribes went through an intensive period of pueblo building, although many of them were abandoned after a few years. The greatest effort of the harassed pueblo builders was at Mesa Verde, where the spectacular ruins testify to the need to fortify for survival. Unfortunately the actual attacks must have taken place away from the protection of the pueblos when the people were working their fields in small groups. By 1300 even Mesa Verde had been abandoned and the pueblo people were concentrated in three main areas—the Hopi villages on Antelope Mesa in Arizona, the Zuñi villages in New Mexico, and the Tanoan and Keresan pueblos on the upper Rio Grande. The southern tribes had been destroyed or were moving into the Sierra Madre Mountains of Chihuahua and Sonora. Aside from the fortlike pueblo settlements, the country was solidly in the hands of the Navajos and the Apaches when Coronado came through in 1540.

During the eighteenth century contact between the whites and the Indians had been made almost everywhere and it is possible to draw a broad picture of the Indians from northern Canada to northern Mexico.

The Eskimos along the far northern coasts had a culture tied to the sea and the hunting of large sea mammals, but the caribou was an important big-game animal during its seasonal migrations. The Athabascan and Algonquian tribes of the northern forests and the tundra country were hunters who depended heavily on the large game mammals—the moose, elk, musk-ox, and, above all, the caribou. In the Northwest, the Indians lived in permanent villages on the salmon rivers and their culture was dependent on harvesting this fish.

In California, there were many large, permanent villages where people lived by seed gathering (especially the acorn), augmented by hunting and fishing. The Great Basin Indians lived as nomads, harvesting piñon nuts in the mountains and various seeds in the deserts. They were skillful hunters of deer, antelope, and mountain sheep. The plateau country drained by the mighty Columbia River is harsh and bleak except along the river courses and here the tribes lived in semipermanent villages, hunting most of the year and fishing during the seasonal salmon runs. In the Southwest, from the upper Colorado and Rio Grande rivers down into Mexico, the tribes continued to depend on agriculture, with corn the most important crop. Even the warlike Navajo did some corn raising but their life was being radically changed by two Spanish innovations—the horse and the domestic sheep. By raiding the ranches the Navajo became horsemen and nomadic herdsmen and the enormous flocks of sheep on their reservations today are still their main food source. In the early 1700's the acquisition of the horse had created a new way of life in the high desert and Great Plains. There the Indians evolved a Plains culture based entirely on buffalo hunting. The horse gave many tribes a mobility they had never dreamed possible. In the Eastern Woodland

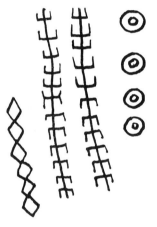

Red painting, Cerro Blanco de Covadonga, Durango. Redrawn from J. Alden Mason, 1961.

Incised animals, Lucerne Valley, southern Wyoming. Redrawn from Russ Grimshaw and Clyde May.

many people left their cornfields and pottery and the beginnings of a sedentary village life to become hunting and fighting nomads on the plains. Wandering hunters from the north and west converged on the grassland with its numberless buffalo now easy to hunt on horseback. Easy access to this inexhaustible food supply made the Plains Indians wealthy and independent.

In the southeastern Woodland where agriculture started about the time of Christ, the growing of corn never assumed the same importance that it had in the Southwest. Forests and streams provided abundant hunting and fishing and the ease of living led to large permanent settlements. Not long before the Spanish encountered them in 1540, these southeastern tribes had acquired some cultural traits that were astonishingly like a watered-down version of those found in the high culture centers of Middle America, including earth pyramids, feather mantles, a well-defined caste system, elaborate carving in stone, and, in certain areas, human sacrifice. Their culture was so far advanced over the northeastern Woodland Indians that they became known as the "Civilized Tribes."

In the northeastern Woodland, agriculture arrived late, about A.D. 1000 in the New England area, and the principal means of sustenance continued to be hunting. By the 14th century, a wedge of Iroquoian-speaking people from the Mississippi Valley had split the great Algonquian bloc as far north as the Saint Lawrence River.

These vigorous newcomers brought some astonishing new ideas. They formed what amounted to an Indian League of Nations, levying tribute from their less organized neighbors and controlling much of the northeastern United States until the coming of the whites. These people practiced agriculture, lived in stockaded villages, and had a social organization reminiscent of the Southeast and Middle America. North of the areas where corn would grow, hunting continued to be the way of life.

This was the picture of the "American Indian" when the white invasions began. These were the complex and varied peoples who painted and engraved the mysterious rock pictures sometime between 10,000 B.C. and the present. In subsequent sections, some partial answers will be given about the creators of rock art in specific areas. Enough data is at hand to make some valid conjectures on the late prehistoric and historic periods, but on the earlier material there is much that can never be known.

2 TECHNIQUES

The terminology of rock art is confusing. In this country, two words—petroglyph (rock engraving) and pictograph (rock painting)—occur frequently in the literature. Some investigators reverse these definitions —others add petrograph and pictoglyph. In Europe the inclusive term is "rock art," with "rock painting" and "rock engraving" the subdivisions. There can be no confusion with this method and several authorities in the United States are now adopting it. In this book, I have mainly followed the European system, using petroglyph and pictograph only where it is more convenient or in reference to published works. Therefore, it will be well to get them straight at the start.

Red painting, Tulare County, California. From photograph by Robert Luthey.

PETROGLYPH—AN ENGRAVING ON STONE

A drawing on stone that is pecked, incised (carved), scratched, or abraded, or a combination of these techniques.

Petroglyphs are the most common form of rock art in North America and they occur by the thousands, especially in the Southwest and the Great Basin area. Most petroglyphs are produced by rock pecking. This can be done in two ways—by striking the surface of the rock with a sharp piece of harder stone or, for more precise control, by chiseling the rock, using a hammer stone to pound on the stone chisel. The design is usually started with a series of dots joined into lines by continued pecking. Flat tones are indicated by close all-over pecking or by abrading the surface (rubbing or scraping with a harder stone).

The three rocks most frequently used are sandstone, volcanic basalt, and granite. All of these, especially in the desert regions, are subject to strong patination, a darkening of the surface caused by oxidization. Over a period of many years, some surfaces become blue-black, an effect

12

known as "desert varnish." When such a patinated surface is broken by the pecking stone, the original much lighter rock color is exposed, giving the design excellent contrast. In rare instances a wall is smoke-blackened and the design is made by removing the blackening over the design areas. In one California site the design is made by cutting through dark lichen to fresh stone.

On some rocks such as the softer sandstones and steatite, designs are incised or carved into the surface and with this technique, the lines are sometimes as deep as an inch or more. Another type of rock art usually listed under gravel petroglyphs is huge figures made on the ground by outlining the shapes with small stones or boulders. In the lower Colorado region of California and Arizona, there are giant animal and human figures made by removing certain stones from areas where all the stones are covered with a dark mahogany-colored desert varnish, thus creating designs in the light sand beneath. These great figures (one is 167 feet long) show up as yellowish-gray figures on a dark brown background. Somewhat similar figures were made in North Dakota, where small rocks were piled up to delineate the design.

PICTOGRAPH–A PAINTING ON STONE

Most of the rock paintings found in North America are painted in various shades of red, ranging from a bright vermilion to a dull brown-red. Sometimes they are in black and rarely in white, while in the regions where polychrome painting was done, a favorite combination was red, black, and white. In a few areas like the Four Corners country of the Southwest, western Texas, and the Chumash territory in southern California, some elaborate polychrome paintings were made with blue, green, and yellow added to the palette.

The enduring pigments used in the rock paintings were earth colors. The red was almost universally made from the iron oxide hematite. Certain tribes, like the Paiute of eastern California, enriched the color by heating the mineral in areas where a naturally brilliant earthy hematite was unavailable. Yellow was made from another iron oxide, limonite, and white from chalky deposits such as diatomaceous earth or minerals like gypsum and kaolin. There were a number of different sources for black, including manganese ore, charcoal, and roasted graphite. The greens and blues were probably derived from one or more of the copper ores so

Pecked animal, possibly a mountain lion, on sandstone, Petrified Forest National Park, Arizona. Photograph by Richard O'Hanlon.

common in the desert country. In some areas where hematite was unavailable, burned clay was ground for pigment. In British Columbia, one method of producing red paint was by baking yellow ochre. In this process, yellow ochre was ground into powder and kneaded with water into balls about the size of walnuts. These were flattened into discs, and baked on a hot fire which converted the yellow ochre into red ochre.[1]

The earthy ores were ground fine in stone mortars and often molded into cakes for storage, to be available for body painting, rock painting, or any decorative use. For rock painting the pigment was reground and mixed with some sort of oil binder to give it permanence. The type of binder certainly varied from place to place but animal oils, blood, white of egg, and vegetable oils were all readily available and any would serve the purpose. The Yokuts of the San Joaquin Valley in California often used sap from the common milkweed *Asclepias* mixed with oil from the crushed seeds of the Chillicothe *Echinocystis*.

The application of the paint to the rock surface was usually done with brushes, some of which have been found in cave shelters. They were made from frayed ends of yucca, twigs or bound masses of fiber like that of the Amole *Chlorogalum*. Pointed sticks may have been used as applicators, and for some of the cruder paintings it is obvious that finger painting did the job. Occasionally the drawing was made directly on the rock with a piece of hematite or a lump of charcoal.

Small paint mortars, sea shells, and the like were used for palettes, and at the larger sites, small depressions were sometimes ground in the rock below the painting to hold colors, traces of which can still be seen.

DISTRIBUTION OF TECHNIQUES

The maps on pages 16 and 17 show the general location of rock-art sites in North America. There are many blanks, especially below the Rio

Grande, where great numbers of sites doubtless exist but the field work in that region has scarcely begun. In the United States only nine states have no recorded rock drawings—Delaware, Florida, Indiana, Louisiana, Mississippi, New Hampshire, New Jersey, South Carolina, and Vermont.

In areas where careful investigations have failed to locate any rock-art sites, there are two basic reasons for the lack—either no appropriate rock surfaces were available or there was no rock-drawing tradition. In Canada sites have been known in British Columbia for many years; more recently, Douglas Leechman and Selwyn Dewdney have been recording the rock art of Alberta, Saskatchewan, Manitoba, and Ontario. I have been able to verify only four sites in Quebec Province, five in Nova Scotia, and one in New Brunswick. So far, no discoveries have been made in Newfoundland or the Yukon.

The four main concentrations of rock art are in California, the Columbia Plateau, the Great Basin region, and the Southwest. The work of recording, especially in the Southwest, is very far from being complete yet several thousands of sites have been recorded. Robert F. Heizer has estimated that there may be 15,000 or more such sites in the western United States. It is not surprising that rock drawings are rare in the Great Plains area but even here paintings and incised drawings are found on the infrequent rock outcroppings. In contrast to the abundance of sites in the West, fewer than 200 rock art sites have been found east of the Mississippi.

The regions where the two basic techniques occur are remarkably well defined. Starting at the extreme northwest part of Alaska, Eskimo incised and pecked designs are found at the few known sites down to and including Kodiak Island. At the Eskimo sites in Cook Inlet and Prince William Sound, the rock art is painted. In southeastern Alaska and the adjoining coastal strip of British Columbia and Washington, the typical northwestern rock art is almost entirely pecked or incised. Inland sites from the Fraser River south to central Oregon and east in a broad zone to eastern Ontario are chiefly painted. In central North America from the Pacific to the Atlantic, pecked or incised designs predominate, with large concentrations of paintings in southern California and Utah. The last region includes southwestern Texas and northern Mexico, and the known sites are mainly painted.

In most of the areas containing rock art, both techniques occur but one or the other form is always dominant. In later chapters where each region is discussed separately, a more detailed breakdown of the two techniques will be shown. Fairly often both painting and carving occur in the same general locality and even at the same site. Rarely the two techniques are combined in the same design with the pecked or incised lines filled in with paint.

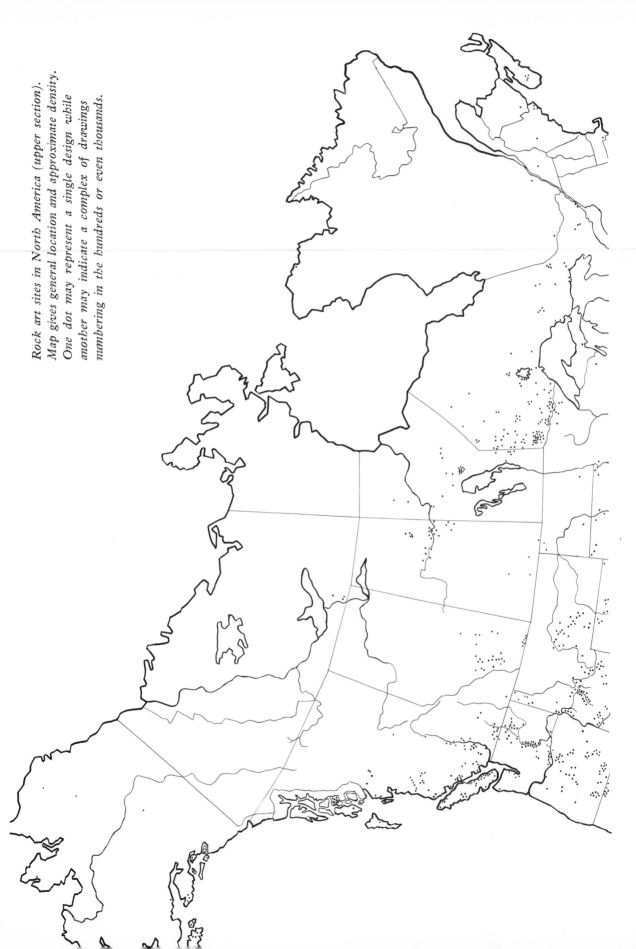

Rock art sites in North America (upper section).
Map gives general location and approximate density.
One dot may represent a single design while
another may indicate a complex of drawings
numbering in the hundreds or even thousands.

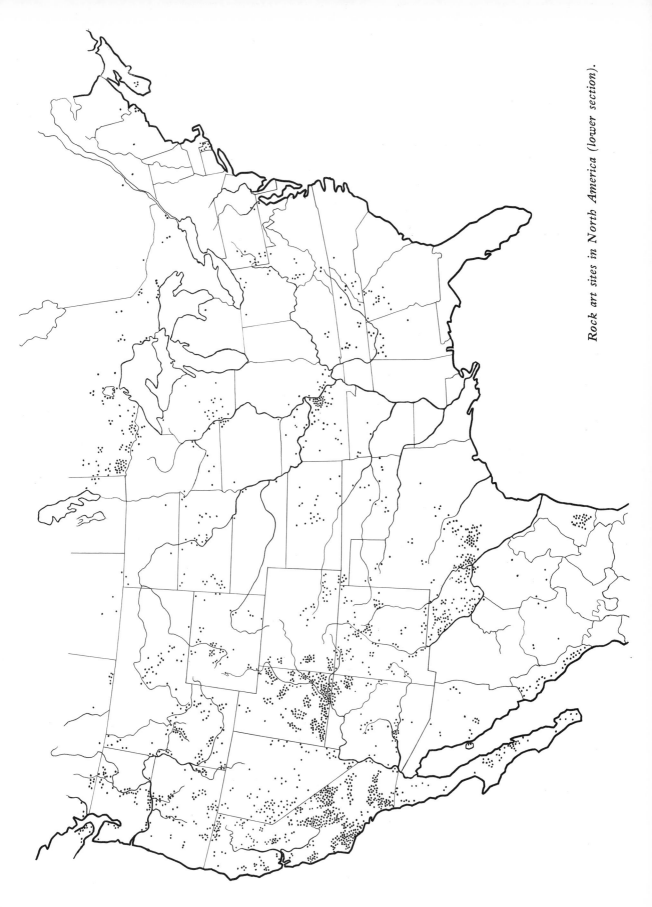

Rock art sites in North America (lower section).

3 STYLES

*Abstract pecking,
Wupatki National Monu-
ment, Arizona.*

In the history of art there has been a noticeable tendency for forms to evolve from naturalistic, through stylized, to abstract. Any major deviation from this pattern is usually due to a strong new influence coming from outside. These art developments have occurred many times in different parts of the world and invariably they have occurred where peoples have been leading a sedentary existence in settled villages and cities. The art of the nomadic hunter on the other hand has a tendency to remain static. For countless centuries, the cave art of Paleolithic man continued to depict the major game animals and very little else. Mesolithic man in eastern Spain added the hunter himself to the scene but the beautiful paintings remained highly naturalistic. With the dawn of agriculture in the Near East, true village life began and new art forms appeared.

This generalization seems to work in the New World as well. The oldest examples of rock art are to be found in the petroglyphs of the Great Basin and the Southwest, where there are often as many as three or four designs superimposed one over the other. Of course it would have been ideal if a rock-art-producing people had lived at the same spot for thousands of years in complete isolation, allowing us to make a perfect reconstruction of their style changes and development. Unfortunately this never happened and we are faced with many puzzles that may never be properly explained. It is important to remember that though the Anasazi people of the Southwest remained in the same general area for a very long time, they were exposed to pressures from the outside and there were many migrations and shifts in population going on in the area, bringing not only new ideas but disruption or destruction of old patterns. Between 1958 and 1961, Christy Turner had a unique opportun-

18

ity to study the petroglyphs of the Glen Canyon area of the Colorado River before it was flooded by the waters of Lake Powell. He was able to distinguish five different styles in a chronological sequence through superimposition, and association with ruins and pottery.[1]

David Gebhard has described four basic styles in his study of the petroglyphs of Wyoming.[2]

Type I	Small realistic animal and human drawings.
Type II	Nonrealistic outlined humanoid forms; animals remain realistic.
Type III	Large panels of highly stylized anthropomorphs; animals remain realistic.
Type IV (Historic)	Typical northern Plains Indian art—realistic humans, animals, especially the horse.

Here is a clear transition from a naturalistic style to an abstract approach, broken in late prehistoric or historic times by encroachment from the east—Plains Indian hunters with their realistic art tradition (although Gebhard has remarked that there is no way to prove that Types I, II, and III were all made by the same people). It is interesting to note that the animal drawings remain realistic through all four periods, reflecting a continuing dependence on hunting and hunting magic.

DISTRIBUTION OF STYLES

PRINCIPAL ROCK-DRAWING STYLES*

The areas in parentheses indicate regions where the style is concentrated. This listing is of necessity a great simplification of the problem. In some areas a number of these styles occur.

Painted	*Pecked or Abraded*	*Incised or Scratched*
Naturalistic (Northern Woodland, Columbia-Fraser Plateau, Southwest)	Naturalistic (Great Basin, Southwest)	Naturalistic (Great Plains)
Naturalistic Polychrome (Southwest, Great Plains)	Stylized (Northwest, Southwest, Great Plains)	
Stylized (California, Southwest)	Abstract Curvilinear (Great Basin)	

Red painting, Meyer Springs, Texas. From photograph by Donald Martin.

* For areas, refer to area map, page 80. The location of styles is shown in greater detail in the chart on page 150.

Painted	Pecked or Abraded	Incised or Scratched
Stylized Polychrome (Southwest)	Abstract Rectilinear (Great Basin, Southwest)	
Abstract Linear (California, Great Basin)	Pit and Groove (California)	
Abstract Polychrome (California)		

Sometimes these terms can be confusing, especially *stylized* and *abstract*. I give my interpretation:

Naturalistic	Done in a realistic or natural manner.
Stylized	Recognizable subjects rendered in a conventionalized or nonrealistic manner.
Abstract	Having little or no reference to the appearance of objects in nature.

At some sites, two or more styles are included in a single panel.

PAINTED (NATURALISTIC)

This style is confined to the regions dominated by a nomadic hunting economy. The paintings are mainly simple, rather crude representations of men and animals. In most areas the drawings are done in red alone, though black and white were sometimes added.

A major concentration is in the lake and river country of the Northern Woodland, where men in canoes, moose, elk, and buffalo are common subjects. There are occasional representations of mythological creatures like the water panther of the Ojibwa and the ubiquitous thunderbird. Some simple abstract elements occur but they are subordinate to the naturalistic style. This style continues westward through the prairies of western Canada to the Columbia-Fraser Plateau. Paintings feature many animals, chiefly deer and mountain sheep, with a few rare fish and buffalo. An abstract element, a semicircle with rays, often occurs with naturalistic forms. Human forms are abundant, especially twin figures, sometimes with linked hands.

An isolated area where naturalistic rock paintings were made is on the Alaskan coast east of Kodiak Island, where the Eskimo painted very simple pictures in red representing killer whales, various land mammals, and humans.[3]

PAINTED (NATURALISTIC POLYCHROME)

The finest examples of this style are found in two small areas in the Southwest. In the Canyon de Chelly, northeastern Arizona, there are

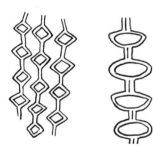

Red painting, Sierra Santa Teressa, Sonora.

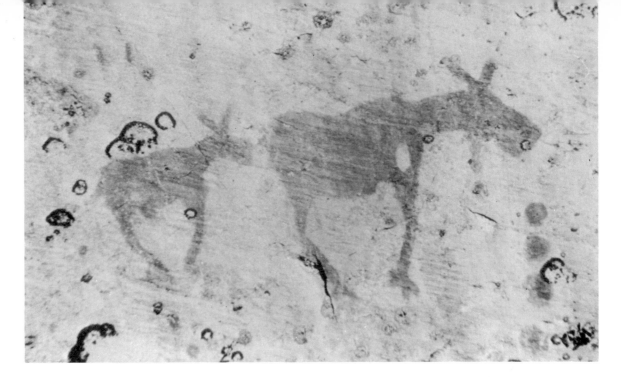

Naturalistic painting in red of cow moose and calf, Darky Lake, Quetico Provincial Park, Ontario. Photograph by Selwyn Dewdney.

many panels featuring horsemen, priests, antelope, and the like. These fine paintings are done by the Navajo and are reminiscent of Plains paintings on buffalo robes. In eastern New Mexico and western Texas there are a few sites with realistic polychrome animals by the Apache.

PAINTED (STYLIZED POLYCHROME)

This handsome style is confined to the Southwest. The best examples are from the Four Corners region, especially northern Arizona and northern New Mexico. The most characteristic figures are the square-shouldered, triangular-bodied *kachina* figures and the textile and pottery designs of the Anasazi. *Kachina* is the Hopi term for supernatural beings impersonated by men wearing masks during tribal ceremonies. The *kachinas* still play an important part in the religious life of these Indians. This style had a wide dispersal in the Southwest and there are examples from southern Nevada to southwest Texas.

Outstanding examples of this style are found in Navajo paintings from Carrizo and Largo canyons in northwestern New Mexico and the Sierra Santa Teressa near Hermosillo, Sonora.

PAINTED (ABSTRACT POLYCHROME)

The only concentration of this style, the finest flowering of rock painting in North America, is in the Santa Barbara-Kern-Tulare regions of

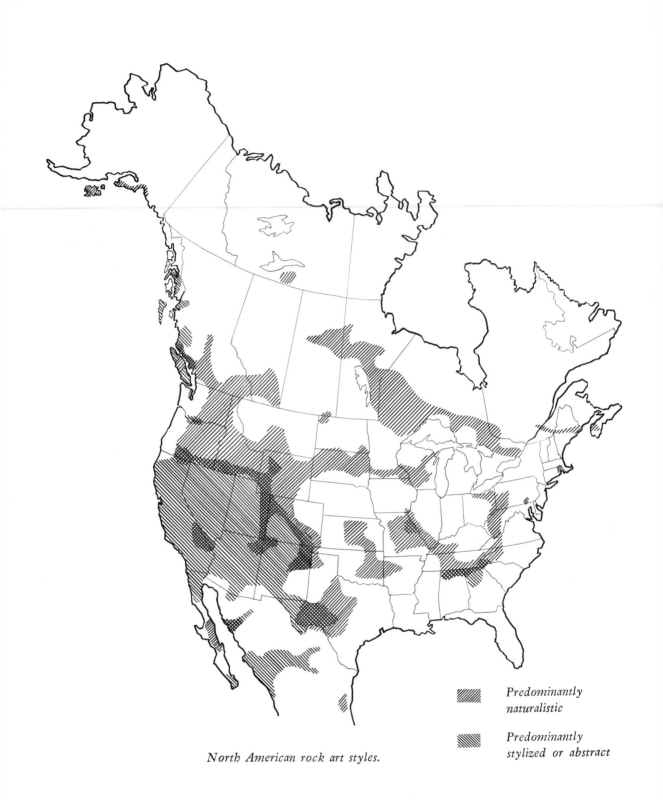

North American rock art styles.

Predominantly
naturalistic

Predominantly
stylized or abstract

California. Basically simple designs like concentric circles are elaborated in the most extraordinary and diverse ways. The main device is to put multiple outlines of contrasting colors around shapes. There is much use of dotted outline both by itself and to add complexity to already complex figures. There are many fanciful anthropomorphic and zoomorphic creatures. The most beautiful paintings are in the coast ranges of the Santa Barbara area but the Kern-Tulare or Sierra Nevada foothill region paintings are so similar in technique that there must have been a considerable exchange of ideas.

PAINTED (ABSTRACT LINEAR)

In the coastal ranges south of Los Angeles, there are many isolated boulders and small rock shelters where simple rectilinear red designs occur. There are few design elements, mainly zigzags, chevrons, and diamonds, and occasionally hand impressions. Along the western edge of the Great Basin (western Nevada and eastern California) there are a few sites with curvilinear designs. The elements are simple—concentric circles, rows of short lines, connected circles and bisected circles. The most striking examples of this style are found near Hermosillo, Mexico, where there are many thin-line drawings of great complexity suggesting textile designs.

Red painting of killer whale, Cook Inlet, Alaska. Redrawn from Frederica de Laguna, 1933.

PECKED (NATURALISTIC)

Of all realistic pecked designs, that of the mountain sheep appears most often and occurs over a very large area. It has been recorded from every mountainous region where the now rare species occurred, from eastern California to Texas and north into Montana. The animal is invariably drawn in profile but often the horns are drawn as if the head were turned to the front. At times just the head is shown front face. Many other animals like the buffalo, deer, coyote, and horse are pecked into sandstone and basaltic rocks. The bear was seldom attempted but was usually represented by the bear track. Human figures are nearly always drawn front view and look rather like gingerbread men. Even when holding a bow and arrow, the figure is rendered front view. On page 24 is a beautiful pecked rendering of a horse. This is probably a late Navajo drawing but is so unlike anything else in the country, it must reflect white-influenced school training. There are naturalistic pecked drawings in the Eastern Woodland featuring men, animals, birds, especially the thunderbird or men in thunderbird costume and many kinds of tracks.

PECKED (STYLIZED)

This type of rock drawing is concentrated in two widely separated regions—the Northwest and the Southwest. The Northwest pecked de-

Abstract linear patterns in red on granite near Poway, California. Photograph from the San Diego Museum of Man.

Pecked naturalistic drawing of a horse, probably Navajo, from the Glen Canyon region of the Colorado River, Utah. Site is now under water. Photograph from the Museum of Northern Arizona.

Stylized pecked figures near Moab, Utah. Photograph by Tom Mulhern.

signs are chiefly of supernatural beings, water monsters, and anthropomorphic figures. A characteristic design is the human head, often drawn without an outline and showing only eyebrows, eyes, nose, and mouth. This design tradition has been adopted by some Eskimo tribes in the region around Kodiak Island. Designs are on granite boulders and of necessity are deeply pecked. Many of the rocks are submerged at every high tide and yet the designs are still clearly visible.

In the Southwest, the most typical designs are *kachina* figures and masks, textile and pottery designs, and "shield" figures rather shallowly pecked on sandstone or basalt. The shield decorated with heraldiclike designs is widespread through the Plains, Southwest, and Great Basin. Often head, arms, and legs are added, giving a Humpty Dumpty effect. In the Fremont culture region of eastern Utah, there are extremely well executed, elaborate figures in ceremonial regalia.

PECKED (ABSTRACT CURVILINEAR)

This style (in which curved lines predominate) is found in both western and eastern United States and Mexico but the greatest concentration is in the Great Basin. The most characteristic form is a sort of aimless

Abstract curvilinear pecked designs, Death Valley, California. Photograph by Donald Martin.

Pecked abstract rectilinear anthropomorphs, Petroglyph Canyon,
Coso Range, California. Photograph by Donald Martin.

Incised naturalistic drawings of horsemen and
shields, Cave Hills, South
Dakota. Photograph from
the South Dakota Depart-
ment of Highways.

Pit-and-groove markings,
west-central Nevada.
Photograph by Donald
Martin.

meandering line, but concentric circles, suns, dotted patterns, clusters of circles, and the like are common. Mountain sheep drawings and representations of *atlatls* are often found associated with this style.

PECKED (ABSTRACT RECTILINEAR)

The abstract rectilinear drawings (predominantly straight lines) are usually found in association with the abstract curvilinear style in the Great Basin and in the Southwest, and the straight-line elements are often superimposed on the curved-line designs and are of a later period. Design elements include rake and ladder shapes, textile designs, grids, various geometric shapes, humans, and bows and arrows. It is interesting to note the naturalistic mountain sheep is very often associated with abstract rectilinear petroglyphs as the only realistic element.

INCISED (NATURALISTIC)

This is the common style in the Northern Plains where the few available areas are of soft rocks, chiefly sandstone. Many of the pictures seem to be late prehistoric or historic and feature horsemen, buffalo, animal and bird tracks, shields and shield figures. The shield motif is recurrent in the Northern Plains as far north as Alberta. Many of the incised rock designs are reminiscent of typical late Plains drawings on skin. There are scattered examples in the Eastern Woodland but the style appears to be a late development reaching its peak after 1750 with the introduction of the horse and the creation of a Plains culture. In a small area in Nova Scotia there are drawings in a unique naturalistic style scratched in smooth slate.

PIT AND GROOVE (ABSTRACT)

These markings hardly qualify as rock art as there is rarely any feeling of pattern. They are circular pits, from one to two inches in diameter, seemingly pecked out of the rock at random, with deeply incised lines around and between the pits. They are rarely found in rock shelters but commonly occur on isolated large boulders. The few examples recorded in central Alberta Province are on glacial erratics—large blocks of quartzite carried south more than 800 miles by glacial action.

The largest number of examples of this style are in west-central California where they are the most abundant type of pecked rocks. In a few instances curvilinear meanders occur with the pit-and-groove elements. In northwestern California, there is one site with bear tracks cut into the stone between the pits, and in one Alberta site a bison head has been added.

4 INTERPRETATION

Pecked figure, Dinwoody Lakes, Wyoming. Redrawn from David Gebhard, 1951.

Interpretation is the most difficult and controversial part of any study of rock drawings. Much of our information has come from living Indians who have taken part in ceremonies involving drawing on rocks or who have copied prehistoric designs. In many instances, however, comments on ancient rock pictures by present-day Indians are highly unreliable; they are apt to tell any fanciful tale to make their questioners happy or to get rid of them. When ceremonial objects, such as masks, that are still in use today but the descendants of the rock-art makers are portrayed, we can be reasonably certain of the significance. Of course we can know only in a general way the reasons for the drawings; precise meanings could come only from the original creators.

CEREMONIAL

The American Indian world was filled with symbolism and mysticism. A complete belief in the spirit world was a guiding factor in all things. Each man had to deal with the plant and animal world every day on the closest terms and his identification with nature was complete. As long as he remained a wanderer and hunter, his religious and ceremonial observances were of the simplest sort. But when he became a village dweller, adopting a sedentary life, the pressure of food gathering lessened and he found himself with more leisure time. He invented complex ceremonies, minor gods around the supreme giver of all good things, and elaborate rituals to communicate with them. Rock drawings were often made in conjunction with ceremonies. Still today the Navajo shamans make symbolic sandpaintings on the ground during healing ceremonies. The ceremonial use of painting continues in northwestern Australia, where the *wondjina* paintings of strange anthropomorphic beings are periodically

28

repainted by the chief of the group under the protection of that particular *wondjina* to assure fertility, rain, increase of animals, and good hunting.[1]

It is certain that great numbers of the rock pictures in North America were made ceremonially to aid in getting all good things—health, fertility, rain, prosperity, and the like. Many of these paintings and engravings were made by the shaman or medicine man, or by tribe members under his direction. The shaman has existed in primitive societies from the days of the sorcerers depicted on the walls of the Paleolithic caves of Europe to the present day. The shaman has the power to communicate between the world of the spirits and the world of men. He can conduct ceremonies to exorcise evil spirits or to appeal for the protection of good spirits. He can also be a physician and officiate at healing ceremonies. A shaman acquires his special power through fasting, isolation, petition to supernatural beings, and by dreaming.

In a number of areas, rock paintings were made in connection with puberty rites. James A. Teit has described the meaning of the paintings made by the Thompson River Indians of British Columbia:

Adolescents of both sexes made records of remarkable dreams, pictures of what they desired or what they had seen, and events connected with their training. These records were made with red paint on boulders and cliffs wherever the surface was suitable . . . Rock paintings were also made by adults as records of notable dreams, and more rarely, of incidents in their lives.[2]

Teit married a Salish woman and lived with these Indians for many years. He knew several Indians who had taken part in such ceremonies and his evidence is thoroughly reliable. At puberty, boys were required to go into the hills on a spirit quest and through praying and fasting, they might have a dream or vision of a supernatural being who would be their guardian and helper in later life. A boy's visions naturally reflected his future hopes. A would-be great warrior hoped that his spirit quest would bring a vision of some aggressive being or force, such as thunder, the sun, grizzly bear, hawk, or eagle. Boys who wanted to be mighty fishermen wanted visions of fish, canoes, ducks, fishing gear, and so on. Gamblers wanted to envision valuables for wagering and aspiring athletes, swift animals and birds. On their return from such an experience, they might be sent to some distant, lonely spot to record their visions on rock with paint.

The girls' puberty ceremony was far more elaborate. They were secluded in a special hut and made to perform many symbolic tasks to ensure industry and ability after marriage. They dug long shallow trenches, collected spruce needles, and wove mats and baskets of grass. It was usual for the girls to bury food where two trails crossed and to hang the mats and baskets they had made on bushes. At the end of their period of seclusion the girls painted representations on rock of the offerings they had made and the tasks they had performed. A few of the symbols painted by the Thompson River girls during the puberty rites are an X, meaning the crossing of two trails; cross-hatched lines, indicating matting; and a curvilinear line with short radiating strokes, representing unfinished basketry.

Among the Nez Percé of Idaho, girls during puberty ceremonies made paintings of objects seen in dreams or connected with the rites. The Quinault boys of Puget Sound made rock paintings during puberty ceremonies and the drawings depicted mythical water monsters seen during their dreams. A rock picture from Quinault territory is shown below. Julian H. Steward, in *Petroglyphs of California and Adjoining States*, described puberty ceremonies as practiced by the Luiseño and Cupeño Indians of southern California:

Among the Luiseño the girls went through an elaborate ceremony at puberty ... This consisted of placing the girls in a pit with heated rocks for three days. On the morning of the fourth day, they left the pit and their faces were painted black for a month. For the second month, vertical white lines were painted on their faces, and for the third month, wavy red horizontal lines. The last was called the "rattlesnake" design. After further ceremonies in which a ground painting was used, the girls had a race to a certain rock. Here relatives of the girls stood to give them red paint when they arrived, and they painted diamond-shaped designs, representing the rattlesnake, on the rock. Among the Cupeño the ceremony is much the same.

This type of design is common in southern California and is almost the only style found over a large area. Here is an example of a southern California puberty drawing.

Rock pictures played a part in fertility ceremonies, and the design element of the bisected circle, considered a fertility symbol in many parts of the world, is abundant in the West. Phallic drawings are frequently

seen at southwestern sites and a fine example is shown here. This amusing rock pecking seems to show, in the clearest posterlike manner, the wish of the male figure for a man-child. In many parts of the West isolated boulders are covered with the distinctive pit-and-groove markings. Such carved boulders are especially abundant in northern California, and in the Pomo territory were known as "baby rocks" and were used ceremonially by women wanting children.

Certain tribes in North Dakota considered the turtle a symbol of productivity and turtle charms were worn by girls hoping for family life and children. Turtle designs have been found pecked and incised on granite boulders in North Dakota and South Dakota and may have represented fertility figures.

In many parts of North America, the shamans had the power to control the weather—to make it rain or to stop the rain. The ceremonies connected with rainmaking reached their greatest elaboration with the Hopi Snake Dance in Arizona. Among the Tolowa, Karok, Hupa, and Shasta Indians in northwestern California, pit-and-groove rocks were used to control the weather.[3]

At one of their fishing places, the Hupa had a sacred rain rock called *mi*. By this rock lived a spirit who could bring frost, prolong the rainy season, or cause drought if he was displeased. When someone was sick or hard frost came, it was thought that someone mourning the death of a relative had passed near the stone and had offended the *mi*. To placate this touchy deity a feast was given and the food was cooked near the rock. The shaman would pray for warm rains to melt the frost while sprinkling the rock with incense-root water. If the end of a rainy spell was needed, powdered incense-root was sprinkled on the rock. The person who had offended the deity was expected to make public apology for passing by the *mi's* dwelling in so unholy a condition.

The Shasta of the Klamath River area believed that long straight parallel grooves would make the snow fall, and to stop a snow storm a scratch was made across and at right angles to the groove. The conical pits produced rain and wind, and the rain could be stopped by covering the rock with powdered incense-root.

The ubiquitous thunderbird motif is connected with the belief that these enormous supernatural birds caused thunder by flapping their wings and lightning by opening and closing their eyes. It has been reported that at the Twana reservation in Washington, there was a carved thunderbird on a basaltic rock and that if the rock was shaken, it would cause rain because the thunderbird was angry. Eastern Woodland carved rocks representing men wearing thunderbird costumes have been recorded, but whether these had any connection with rainmaking rites is unknown.

Pecked figures, Navajo Reservoir, New Mexico. Redrawn from Polly Schaafsma, 1963.

Puberty rites painting in red on granite, San Jacinto Mountains, California. University of California photograph.

Wherever naturalistic animal rock pictures are found, it is almost certain they were made as hunting magic or to increase the supply of game. Very often the animals are depicted pierced with arrows or spears. In the Northern Plains of Alberta, there are a few drawings of buffalo and other big-game animals. Some of these have been found on cliffs at buffalo jumps (high cliffs over which the animals were stampeded).

Robert Heizer and Martin Baumhoff in a recent study of the rock art of Nevada and eastern California state their belief that most of the rock art in Nevada was created in connection with communal hunts for deer, antelope, or mountain sheep. They have located many large petroglyph sites on known migration trails and in narrow draws leading to water. The remains of stone blinds and fences used in sheep or deer ambushes are found near some sites. Other sites are on game trails in areas ideal for antelope corrals. They noted the almost total absence of rock pictures in areas unsuitable for taking game. It is known that among recent Great Basin tribes, a hunt-shaman often directed the communal hunt and it seems likely many of the pictures were pecked by the shaman himself or under his direction prior to the hunt.

According to Edward L. Keithahn,[4] the Tlingit petroglyphs on the Northwest coast are usually located on beach boulders near the mouths of sockeye-salmon streams and are placed so that they face the sea and are submerged at high tide. He thinks that they were made to insure or increase the salmon runs by supernatural means. They often depict such deities as the raven, killer whale, and sea monster.

Pecked drawing of sea monster, Wrangell Island, Alaska. Redrawn from a photograph by Edward L. Keithahn.

There are many rock paintings of sea and land mammals and hunters in boats in Cook Inlet and Prince William Sound, Alaska. An Eskimo has said that they were made by whale killers on the rocks of secret places to brink luck. Another informant said they were made by persons who wanted to become shamans. The student shamans would speak to the paintings and give them offerings of food and clothing. Shortly thereafter they were ready to become full-fledged shamans.[5] It is a practice among the present-day Ojibwa of Lake-of-the-Woods, Ontario, to leave offerings of clothing, tobacco, and prayer sticks on the rocks below a painted rock.[6]

The use of masks and the impersonation of supernatural beings are common to the ceremonies of aboriginal man in all parts of the world. The Eskimo of northern Quebec Province made rock carvings of masks on steatite boulders and the curious nonoutlined faces from Kodiak Island and the Chugach faces from Prince William Sound may also be masks. According to H. I. Smith, the petroglyphs near the present village of Bella Coola, British Columbia, representing the faces of anthropomorphic beings, were made in connection with winter secret society

Design suggesting kachina *mask, Glen Canyon region of the Colorado River, Utah. Site now under water. Museum of Northern Arizona photograph.*

ceremonials where members would pound on them while singing. In the Southwest, particularly the Galisteo Basin in New Mexico, there are rock drawings of *kachina* masks similar to those in kiva murals, some of which are used in present-day Pueblo ceremonies. In northern New Mexico there are beautiful polychrome *yei* figures done by the Navajo that closely resemble supernatural beings personated in the Yebitchai ceremony. The masked *yeis* were closely modeled after the *kachinas* of the Hopi. The early Spanish explorers entering the Southwest in the second half of the sixteenth century described elaborate wall paintings in some of the pueblos and remains of these remarkable ceremonial paintings at Awatovi and Kuaua have been recovered in surprisingly good condition. These complex and beautiful polychrome paintings of anthropomorphic and zoomorphic beings were probably created some time between 1300 and 1500, the ultimate flowering of an art tradition that had been developing as rock art over a very long period. As the ceremonial life of the Pueblo Indians came more and more to revolve around the kiva, there was undoubtedly a lessening of the importance of the rock painting or carving.

The extraordinary and complicated rock paintings in the Santa Barbara–Tulare region of California were certainly created for ceremonial use. In the Chumash area, there are caches of ceremonial objects in the immediate vicinity of painted sites, and in the Yokuts territory, Indian informants have said that the paintings were usually made at a place where ceremonies were performed and that ceremonial objects were often hidden near the paintings. At a major site in the Chumash area, a continuous frieze of paintings 200 feet long is located around the base of a huge natural rock amphitheater rising some 75 feet from the plain. Deep trails cut into the stone lead to the summit where hundreds could sit and look down into the painted section below. It takes little imagination to envision the impressive rituals that must have taken place at this great site.

The Indians of certain areas believed in a number of very special supernatural beings who had great power to help bring about hoped-for results. In the Chumash country of southern California, the people prayed to Sup or Chupu, the giver of all good things. We do not know what this powerful deity looked like but the shamans may have personified him in a variety of ways—there are a number of very potent-looking anthropomorphic figures in the region.

The beautiful polychrome Chumash paintings are almost invariably located in remote, mountainous areas, away from the main population centers along the coast. It is possible that these painted sites are connected with dream or vision quests so important to the American Indian, and that some of these paintings represent such visions. Most of the southern California tribes used the hallucinogenic drug *toloache* or jimsonweed in certain ceremonies, particularly puberty and initiation rites. The root of this common plant was ground and boiled making a liquor that was drunk by ceremony participants. Many of the fanciful Chumash designs may have been produced under the influence of this aboriginal LSD.

In the Great Lakes country and the upper Mississippi Valley, several tribes worshiped a curious being known by many names, such as water panther, water monster, water lynx, and medicine animal. This is usually depicted on rocks and birch-bark scrolls as a clawed animal in profile with a horned head turned full face and a serrated tail curving around the body. This fanciful creature was known to the Ojibwa as *Mishipizhiw*. In 1673, Father Marquette described such a figure painted on a cliff near the present city of Alton, Illinois:

While skirting some rocks, which by their height and length inspire awe, we saw upon one of them two painted monsters which at first made us afraid, and upon which the boldest savages dare not long rest their eyes. They are as large as a calf: they have horns on their heads like those of a deer, a horrible look, red eyes, a beard like a tiger's, a face somewhat like a man's, a body covered with scales, and so long a tail that it winds all around the body, passing above the head and going back between the legs, ending in a fish's tail. Green, red, and black are the three colors composing the picture.

Incised Winnebago drawing of medicine animal (chalked), northeastern Nebraska. Nebraska State Historical Society photograph.

This extraordinary picture could not have been very old as another missionary coming down the Mississippi in 1699 noted that the figures were almost obliterated. Marquette's description would indicate that what he saw was exactly like the medicine animal of the Winnebago. In 1838 one of the figures was still visible but in 1847 the whole face was quarried away. The present painting is the third re-creation of Marquette's creature, each more fanciful than the last. A local sign company is responsible for the most recent effort. It is 50 feet long and bears no relationship whatsoever to any Indian painting style.

Much additional material on ceremonial interpretation and the relation of rock drawings to myths will be found in Part II, on Rock Art Areas.

MNENOMIC

Lacking a written language, aboriginal man has long used pictures as memory aids. With them he recorded objects, concepts, legends, tallies, and records of time. In historic times the Dakota Indians had winter counts as a system of chronology. The record was kept on a buffalo hide. Each year or winter was indicated by a drawing symbolizing some outstanding event, such as an outbreak of smallpox, a successful horse raid, or the death of a chief. In the event of another outbreak of smallpox, the same symbol would be used. Many incised rock drawings in the Great Plains region are done in the same style as the winter-count drawings. The Ojibwa kept track of the order of their ceremonial songs

by symbolic pictures on birch-bark scrolls. The illustrations would give the order of the stanzas and the subject matter of each particular stanza, and the subject matter would be a reminder of the words.

Modern Hopi interpret a number of Arizona petroglyphs as records of the four legendary Hopi migrations of the clans. At many rock drawing sites, there are numbers of short straight vertical lines sometimes in association with animal drawings. It has been suggested that these represent tally marks to record how many animals were taken. It is also possible that each actual drawing of the animal might represent a kill, but lacking ethnographical information, this is pure speculation. In the Southwest there are many carefully pecked designs, suitable for blankets, pottery, and sandals, that look like records for future reference.

RECORDS OF IMPORTANT EVENTS

In the Great Plains region and in the Northern and Eastern Woodlands, there was a tradition of making drawings to commemorate important happenings, usually connected with warfare. The Plains records are almost invariably on skin, but occasionally incised or painted on stone. There is an incised rock panel on the Milk River in southern Alberta that looks like a battle scene: 30 men with guns, 45 other figures, 22 tepees, and 9 horses, some harnessed to travois. In 1852, Henry Schoolcraft described how an Ojibwa, Chingwauk, drew on birch bark for him the record of a successful warlike raid across Lake Superior by a south shore shaman-warrior named Myeengum. The drawings showed Myeengum, his clan symbol, the various legendary beings—like the great serpent and the fabulous water panther—that would aid him in his venture, the five canoes carrying his warriors, three suns to indicate that the passage took three days, and various other symbols. Chingwauk told Schoolcraft that the original painting was made on a cliff of the north shore of Lake Superior. In 1958, over 100 years later, Selwyn Dewdney found the paintings at Agawa Rock exactly as indicated on the birch-bark scroll.

Some Tlingit rock drawings seem to have been made as records of property sacrificed at potlatches or as records of other important events.

The potlatch ceremony practiced by all Northwest Indians was an unusual business. The most important aspect of the Northwest Coast culture was the endless preoccupation with social status and the manipulation of wealth. A chief would give an elaborate feast called a potlatch to celebrate the coming of age of a grandchild, the erection of a house or a totem pole, the birth of a son, and so forth. Many guests were invited and they were obliged to bring many gifts. In the course of the celebrations that might last several days and included feasting, dancing, and other entertainment, the chief would give away slaves, blankets, coppers, canoes, and other valuable property to his guests, who could not decline the presents. The receiver of gifts was obligated to return them with interest at a later time. The host would often ruin a rival by presenting him with far more than he could repay or by publicly destroying much valuable property, which put the rival under the obligation of destroying an equal amount to escape humiliation. This prestige madness was carried to the point where a host would destroy coppers valued at ten thousand blankets each, or burn his canoes and house. The coppers were sheets of copper made in the form of a shield about two feet wide by three feet long. These sheets were often painted with a design or the crest of the owner and were the ultimate in visible signs of wealth.

On the Nass River, British Columbia, there is a painted cave featuring 14 coppers and on the Skeena River near Prince Rupert there is a rock face with six coppers, four with crests and a large anthropomorphic head. These two sites are both in Tsimshian territory. On Petley Point, in Kwakiutl territory, there is a painting showing coppers, boats, and animals.

Recorded at two sites in the White Mesa region of northern Arizona are almost identical drawings, one painted and the other pecked, that may be records of an astronomical phenomenon. Each drawing depicts a crescent shape over a round shape and the astronomer Fred Hoyle has raised the possibility that the Pueblo Indians once occupying the area might have witnessed the supernova of A.D. 1054. On July 4 of that year, Japanese and Chinese astronomers saw an extremely bright nova that was easily visible in broad daylight. This famous supernova, believed to be the origin of the Crab Nebula, was about six times as bright as Venus and was probably the brightest starlike object ever recorded. Astronomers have been able to determine that on July 4, 1054, the moon was in crescent phase directly over and close to the supernova, exactly as shown in the rock drawings. Archaeologists have verified an Indian occupation of the area between 900 and 1100. Representations of stars and planets have been noted in northern Arizona and southern California, and at an elaborate site near Los Angeles there are paintings that could have been inspired only by comets or shooting stars.

Red painting of Mishi-pizhiw, the fabulous night panther, Lake Superior Provincial Park. Redrawn from Selwyn Dewdney, 1962.

Incised battle scene, Milk River, Alberta. Redrawn from Selwyn Dewdney, 1964.

CLAN SYMBOLS

An American Indian clan is an intratribal group, related by blood and organized to promote its social and political welfare. The clan is named for the totem animal or object that is considered its guardian spirit. This is not to be confused with the personal guardian spirit obtained by the individual during puberty dreams and trances. The membership in a clan is usually inherited at birth and the individual is identified during his lifetime as a member of the Bear Clan or the Eagle Clan or the Oak Clan—the possibilities are almost endless. Each clan has one or more symbols to represent the clan.

Many of the often repeated designs found pecked in the rocks, particularly in the Southwest, are clan symbols. At Willow Springs near Tuba City, Arizona, there are sandstone boulders covered with drawings of many different elements. There are repeats of each element, usually neatly arranged in a row. Modern Hopi Indians are able to recognize all but a few of these as clan symbols. Each symbol records that a member of that particular clan passed by that way on a trip from the Hopi villages to collect salt at the springs near the junction of the Colorado and the Little Colorado. The great canyon is regarded with awe by the Hopi—from its depths the ancient Hopi emerged and back to these depths the dead return. From ancient times the Indians have made the journey to get salt from the mysterious and dreaded canyon—only the brave would undertake the trip—and it was natural they would want to commemorate their daring.[7]

Two typical clan symbols are the bear track, always drawn to show the pads and curved claws of the grizzly, the device of the Bear Clan, and the grotesque humped-back flute player, emblem of the Flute Clan.

Animal and thunderbird figures on birch-bark scrolls of the prehistoric woodland Indians like the Ojibwa and the Menomini closely resemble petroglyphs at several western Wisconsin rock shelters. The principal use of the symbols by some historic tribes was as memory aids for the order of songs and dances in various ceremonies and these were inscribed on birch bark or the mnemonic boards of the shamans. In addition, such symbols, especially the thunderbird, were drawn on early land treaties of the Menomini during the 1790's in place of a signature.

DOODLING AND COPYING ANCIENT DESIGNS

A small number of the rock pictures were doubtless done as a form of amusement and to while away an idle hour. Such aimless rock pictures were certainly confined to pecked or incised designs. The preparation of materials for making a rock painting (see chapter 2) would hardly

Red painting of crescent and round shapes, possibly representing supernova of 1054 A.D., White Mesa, Arizona. From photograph by William C. Miller.

Pecked Hopi clan symbols (chalked), Willow Springs, Arizona. Some of the clans represented on this rock are the Cloud, Coyote, Spider, Corn, and Rope. Museum of Northern Arizona photograph.

appeal to the rock doodler but implements to peck a design into the rock—a hammer stone and a flint chisel—were ready at hand almost anywhere.

There is ethnographic evidence that some crude pictures were done by children and others were copies of older examples on the same rock surface "made for fun" by recent Indians with no knowledge of their meaning. In the Great Basin area of California there are obviously old designs, half obscured with patination, next to identical fresh designs.

5 ROCK ART AS ART

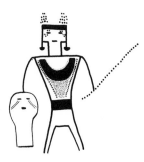

Pecked figure near Vernal, Utah. From photograph by John Cawley.

Since "art for art's sake" was not the main consideration in the mind of the Indian creators and the pictures on the rocks were put there for special purposes, usually ceremonial, to many American archaeologists the art aspect of rock pictures is secondary and to some nonexistent.

The art historian takes exception to this narrow point of view. He notes that nearly all the ancient arts in the world were motivated by religion. The superb ritualistic carvings, paintings, and metal work of Egypt are certainly art. The temple figures of the Greek gods, personifications of supernatural beings, are universally considered art. There are many examples of rock art, such as those featuring crude stick figures or curvilinear meanders, that no one would classify as art; but the moment an aboriginal craftsman bothered to pick out a particularly smooth and colorful piece of rock on which to peck a carefully conceived and decorative figure, you are dealing with an artist. True, he may have been a tribal shaman whose main concern was to put down a visualization of a certain supernatural being for ceremonial use, but if he was concerned in the least with composition, design, or craftsmanship, his work has to be considered art. This has long been recognized in Europe where the study of rock paintings and carvings has been in the hands of art historians as well as archaeologists. In the great mass of European publications on the subject, it is referred to as rock art and the familiar American terms of petroglyph and pictograph are unknown.

Only during periods of prosperity and freedom from want has man had the leisure to develop great art. In North America, rock pictures usually attained the stature of art in those areas where a nomadic hunting culture had been supplanted by a stable sedentary culture nurtured by an abundant food supply near at hand. These qualifications are met in

40

the salmon-economy villages of the Northwest, the fishing and acorn-gathering settlements of the Santa Barbara–Tulare region in California, and the corn-growing villages of the Southwest. In these three areas, North American rock art reaches its highest development.

There seem to be three stages in the development of a rock-art tradition:

1. The primitive hunters and food gatherers. These people have no fixed villages and constantly move about seeking game or seed crops. Their ceremonies consist chiefly of healing rites, taboos, and super-stitions, and their rock drawings are mainly crude representations of game animals, hunters, and a few mythological beings. Indians like the Ojibwa never got beyond this stage.

2. The primitive village dwellers. They can be hunters, food gatherers, or primitive agriculturists but their sedentary life has allowed them the leisure to develop regular ceremonial practices and art styles. Typical of this stage are the Chumash of California and the Fremont culture in Utah. The finest rock art was developed by Indians at this culture stage.

3. The highly developed village dwellers. These people have .evolved elaborate ceremonies and pantheons of gods, and their best artistic efforts are no longer found on rocks. Better and more convenient surfaces are used with more sophisticated results. Three outstanding examples of this higher culture stage are the superb carvings on wood and stone of the Northwest Indians, the kiva and sand paintings of the Hopi and Navajo in the Southwest, and the Mexicanized art in wood, copper, and shell of the Southeast. In all of these areas, rock drawings had ceased to play a major part by the start of the historic period. Of the three, only the Southwest had a long rock-art tradition.

The great variation in quality of Indian rock pictures is the result of two factors. The most obvious, of course, is that individuals differ enor-mously in ability. More important is the rare appearance of a forceful person with original ideas and talent who sets a new art style that is accepted and imitated over a wide area.

It is curious that the hunting people of the New World who painted and carved thousands of naturalistic animal forms on rocks across the continent never approached the excellence of the Paleolithic cave painters of southern France and northern Spain. It is not that they were incapable of doing that sort of work, but that they simply did *not* do it. There are several possible explanations for this. The European paintings were made over a very long period of time during the last great ice age. The pop-ulation above and below the Pyrenees must have been remarkably sparse 30,000 years ago and the small bands of hunters were undoubtedly con-centrated in and around the numerous deep caves in the glacier-covered regions. The deposits found in the caves and rock shelters testify to long occupation that allowed ample time in one spot for the development of their distinct high art form. At a very early period, a highly naturalistic painted art tradition was developed, probably sparked by a single highly gifted individual. (Such a person was Giotto, the first great painter of the Italian Renaissance.) The similarity of technique in nearly all the sites has often been remarked on. Down through the years, the older drawings were held up as models and the technique remained unchanged. Paleolithic man was a conservative—his flint tools underwent little change for many thousands of years and the same seems true of his approach to art.

The nomadic hunters of the New World plains and woodlands, unhampered by perpetual snow and ice, pursued the migrant game herds and seldom stayed long in any one place. Theirs was a life of constant change and movement with no hope of acquiring the leisure necessary for the development of a higher art form. Occasionally a site is discovered in the hunting country with a far better than average animal drawing. Given the opportunity, the individual who created it might have been the nucleus of an art tradition.

The Athabascan nomads who infiltrated the Southwest plateau country and came to be known as the Navajo acquired rather rapidly most of the ceremonial and artistic traditions of the Pueblo people. These borrowed ideas flowered under the hands of the clever Navajo into the highly developed art tradition we know today. Their excellent polychrome rock paintings in northern New Mexico seem midway in style between the Pueblo kiva figures and the highly stylized Navajo sandpainting anthropomorphs.

Black painting, Baja California. From photograph by Velma Pontoni.

6 DATING

Determining the age of prehistoric paintings and carvings is difficult and absolute datings are rare. A number of dating methods can give partial answers. Some give relative chronologies so that in a given area it can be determined which drawings are older. Other methods give approximate datings, give or take a hundred years or so. In a very small number of cases the age of the rock art can be exactly stated.

Some North American rock pecked designs are in all likelihood far older than any existing paintings. Rock paintings are made on boulders, on cliff faces, and in shallow rock shelters where most of them are under constant wind and water attack. Under these conditions few could be older than several hundred years. On the other hand, designs pecked into dense basaltic rock could endure for thousands of years. The conditions that protected the Paleolithic paintings in Europe for so many thousands of years in great underground caverns did not exist in this country.

Red painting, Real County, Texas. Redrawn from A. T. Jackson.

BY PATINATION

Most of the rock drawings in the Great Basin and in the Southwest are made by pecking through the dark patina or "desert varnish" to the original lighter rock color. Desert varnish is a blackish or brownish stain of hydrous iron and manganese oxides on rock surfaces. It is most conspicuous in desert regions but is also found in rain forests and at high altitudes. Although the pecked designs are nearly all on the sandstone and basaltic rock so common in the western desert, desert varnish occurs on almost any kind of rock. There are various theories to account for its formation. One attributes it to rain water that has soaked into the rock and then been brought back to the surface through capillary action.

The water brings various chemicals in the rock, such as carbonates, sulphates, and oxides, to the surface. Some of these tend to darken and harden the surface of the stone. In addition to the darkening caused by deposition of soluble chemicals, there seems to be a darkening due to the action of direct sunlight.[1]

Another theory is that ample sunlight and moisture were needed for the formation of the conspicuous deposits of desert varnish on the Colorado plateaus and the principal deposits must have been formed during pluvial periods, making the older varnish perhaps as old as the late Wisconsin glacial, ten to fifteen thousand years ago.[2] According to this theory, desert varnish is being formed at a very slow rate today in the Southwest where rainfall is scanty. The new desert-varnish deposits are restricted to places that are often wet. Boulders along the Colorado River between high- and low-water stages are stained a very dark brown. In California, petroglyphs on granite rocks below high-water mark in the Kern River Gorge have turned an intense black.

Donald Martin of Santa Rosa, California, who has devoted much time to the study of western rock art and particularly to the problem of desert varnish has a different idea. He has taken heavily patinated stones from the Mojave Desert back to Santa Rosa, located in the coastal ranges where the summers are hot, the winters cold, and the yearly rainfall averages over 30 inches. After two years of exposure in this climate, all patina had vanished from the stones. This would indicate that desert varnish could not have formed during periods of unusual rainfall.

If Martin's hypothesis is correct, the Mojave Desert basaltic rocks were patinated during and after the decline of the last great rainy period, the "Little Pluvial" of some 3,000 or 4,000 years ago. Thus no designs pecked on such rocks could be more than 2,000 to 3,000 years old.

For arriving at relative chronologies through a study of patination, it is necessary to have varying degrees of desert varnish on petroglyphs at the same site. The older the carving, the darker the patina. At many sites, some of the pecked areas are identical in patination and weathering to the natural rock surface; others that are known to be at least 150 years old look as fresh as if they had been pecked yesterday. At the present time there is no way to determine the rate of patination, but totally patinated designs may be several thousand years old.

BY SUPERIMPOSITION OF STYLES

Often one design has been pecked over another—the superimposed drawing done later than the partially obliterated underdrawing. Sometimes three or more designs in differing styles are layered in a recognizable sequence. Patination and weathering are useful additional clues to separate these multiple superimpositions. Once the sequence of styles has been established, a yardstick is created to judge relative chronology of styles anywhere in the region, even where no superimposition occurs. For example, in the Great Basin area, the rectilinear abstract style is often found over the curvilinear abstract style and is more recent. The curvilinear abstract drawings are almost invariably found beneath the other styles and can be safely designated the earliest Great Basin style. One of the arguments in favor of a fairly recent dating for the rock paintings in California is the rather rare occurrence of superimposition. Of the 80 sites recorded in the Chumash region, only six show such evidence.

Where designs are pecked or painted over designs of a similar style, there is the possibility we are dealing with a single period in time and the superimposition represents deliberate obliteration. The Hopi ceremonial kiva paintings were periodically covered wth plaster and new designs applied. The Kuaua kiva had 87 layers of plaster, 25 of which were painted with elaborate mural designs.[3] The Navajo sand paintings, destroyed after each ceremony, demonstrate ritual obliteration.

Pecked figure, Petroglyph Canyon, Coso Range, California. From photograph by John Cawley.

BY RADIOCARBON TEST

The radiocarbon method of dating organic materials was developed by Dr. Willard Libby at the Institute of Nuclear Physics, University of Chicago, and has been particularly valuable in dating American Indian remains. Carbon 14 (a radioactive isotope of carbon) is formed in the atmosphere when cosmic rays bombard nitrogen atoms. All living things absorb carbon 14 at a constant rate, but at death, the absorption stops and the carbon 14 atoms start disintegrating at a known and steady rate. After $5,760 \pm 30$ years have elapsed, half the carbon 14 atoms have dis-

Horsemen and sheep, Arches National Monument, Utah. Photograph by Tom Mulhern.

integrated. A sample of the organic material to be dated is purified and processed through apparatus that filters out background radiation. The number of beta particles given off per minute, measured by a Geiger-counter technique, determines the amount of radioactive material left in the sample, and consequently the approximate date at which the sample ceased to be a living organism. The method allows for a margin of error in each direction, and radiocarbon dates are often written like this: 2,700 B.P. (before present) ± 220 years.

This dating method has been applied to rock art but without much success so far. I recently collected some paint samples from a badly eroded site near Santa Barbara, hoping that enough of the original organic paint binder remained for radiocarbon dating. Unfortunately the sample was too small for a conclusive dating but the laboratory report indicated no great age. I then tried dating basketry fragments from a painted cave. The sample proved to be 120 ± 80 years old. Clement Meighan has dated a palm-wood peg from a painted cave in Baja California that proved to be 530 ± 80 years old. The dating of associated artifacts can never give an absolute dating for the rock drawings but it does indicate a period when the site was occupied by people who *might* have made the pictures.

BY OVERGROWTH OF LICHENS

Many petroglyph sites have design areas partially covered with lichens, and various investigators have discussed dating such sites by establishing the age of the extremely slow-growing lichens on the pecked surfaces. The recent studies by Ronald E. Beschel on the growth rates of Arctic lichens have provided the methods for such dating.[4] The growth rate varies greatly depending on the species, type of rock, and climate. The periods when the growth conditions of water, warmth, light, and food are favorable are very short in most areas, and some of the crust lichens grow as little as a fraction of a millimeter in diameter per year.

Growth rates have been arrived at through actual measurements (the longest observed lichen growth covers only about 40 years) and comparisons with lichens of known age. In the latter case, it is necessary to know when a rock was first exposed to the air-borne lichen spores. This is possible with certain volcanic rocks, rocks turned up during old road-building operations, gravestones, rocks emerging from drained lakes, and the like.

Through studying the growth of lichens, maximum ages have been determined for a number of species (around 700 years in several instances). On the basis of present knowledge, lichen growth-rates can be used to date sites later than the approximate 700-year lichen age limit. Beschel has estimated the age of one lichen-encrusted Eskimo site as "at

Incised drawing of cranes, Gullickson Glen, Wisconsin. From photograph by Warren Wittry.

least 500 years" and Gerhard Folmann, using Beschel's methods, has recently given an average age of 430 years to the great rock figures on Easter Island.[5] It is obvious that this method has great possibilities for solving dating problems in regions where favorable lichen growth conditions are found.

BY DEPOSITS COVERING DESIGNS

Robert F. Heizer and Martin A. Baumhoff have described three Nevada sites where rock drawings occur in association with alluvial deposits and occupation debris that give some dating clues.[6]

In the first instance, the designs are pecked on a cliff above an alluvial terrace of gravel. Excavation of the terrace disclosed buried petroglyphs extending to a depth of over twenty feet. The terrace is part of a large alluvial fan formed by a small intermittent stream and a gradual accumulation of the deposit is indicated by the stratification of the sand and gravel into thin, even beds. The annual rainfall of the region averages two and a half inches, indicating a very long time for the building of the terrace.

At another site, a large red *kachina* figure was buried up to the shoulders by four or five feet of camp debris. This amount of debris in a rock shelter would indicate several hundred years of occupation and at least that age for the painting.

The third instance is somewhat different. Here the pecked designs are in a large rock shelter and above an accumulation of 20 feet of deposit. The upper levels of this shelter contained materials of cultures dating from historic times to around 1000 B.C., while the lowest-level materials date from about 4000 B.C. As the drawings could not have been made until the debris reached its present level, they must have been made within the last 3,000 years.

BY RATE OF EROSION

All rock drawings are exposed to the destructive forces of erosion but the rate of this erosion can vary enormously. Fine-grained rocks like basalt and quartzite are highly resistant to erosion while the coarse sandstones are very susceptible to wind and water damage. Rock paintings are far more apt to be destroyed through erosion than are pecked and carved designs, and the Indian craftsmen, aware of this problem, almost invariably did their painting in rock shelters where there was maximum protection from the scouring effects of wind-blown sand and rock-destroying moisture. On the other hand, nearly all rock-pecked drawings are on exposed cliff faces and individual rocks.

There is a site in the Nojoqui Valley, near Santa Barbara, that was pictured in Mallery's book (1893) with five pages of polychrome geometric patterns. Today there is hardly a trace of the painting to be seen. The cave entrance faced the prevailing wind and the paint was literally sand-blasted away. These paintings could not have been over several hundred years old. Mallery also pictured the Painted Cave on nearby San Marcos Pass. This well-known painting is still exactly as it was in 1893. In this instance, the cave opening allowed the wind to strike a six-foot-wide section of the painting. This section has been obliterated, dividing the picture into two parts. The Mallery paintings show that this destruction had already taken place over seventy years ago.

BY ASSOCIATION WITH ARTIFACTS

Indian artifacts found near rocks with pecked designs or painted caves can sometimes be used to indicate approximate dating. In the Sierra Madre back of Santa Barbara, California, many objects of bone, wood, and shell, typical of the late Chumash culture, have been found in rock shelters near painted sites. At a number of these sites, Spanish beads and other postcontact material have been recovered. The evidence would indicate that the paintings are relatively recent and that the practice of rock painting continued in this area at least until the start of the Spanish-mission period.

In the Pueblo areas of northern Arizona and New Mexico, artists sometimes stood on the house roofs in order to paint or carve designs on the rock wall above. Emil Haury has described a site in northeastern Arizona where paintings occur on the wall of an overhanging cliff. Against the cliff are a number of houses built in contact with the rock wall, a practice followed only in late Pueblo times (A.D. 1200–1300). Many paintings were made from these roof tops and the most common design element was the hand (see chapter 7). Since the Pueblo Indians had abandoned the area to the Navajos by 1300, it is reasonable to assume that these designs were made prior to that date. There is one cut timber from the site with a tree-ring date of 1247. The later Navajo drawings are shallow scratchings on the cliff face, mostly of animals and horsemen.

The best correlation of prehistoric artifacts with rock drawings has been made by Christy G. Turner. When the Glen Canyon region of the Colorado was threatened with inundation by the creation of Lake Powell, a salvage program to record several hundred archaeological sites was undertaken. Pecked designs were found at many sites in association with pottery that has been dated and ascribed to specific cultures.[7] Turner's assumption that the rock pictures are contemporaneous with the pottery seems valid. His dates for the drawings are from before A.D. 1050 to late historic times.

Most American Indians deny any knowledge of the rock drawings or their creators. Ute and Southern Paiute Indians have said the pictures were made by supernatural beings or by ancient peoples or by animals when they were men. Some Idaho Indians ascribe the designs to the medicine men, who were the only people who could interpret their meaning. Other Idaho Indians hold that the rock pictures were made by mythical creatures or that they fell from the sky. Modern Pueblo Indians sometimes carve symbols on rocks and some of the clan symbols described in chapter 4 were made not many years ago, according to Hopi informants. Ute Indians admit to copying old designs whose meaning was unknown to them "just for fun," while the Western Yavapai of Arizona sometimes made petroglyphs in imitation of ancient ones.

In chapter 4 on interpretation, there are descriptions of the puberty-rites paintings made by some Salish tribes in British Columbia and the Luiseño in southern California. Women have been interviewed who actually painted such pictures in the late 19th century. These two areas are unique in giving us exact information on how these pictures were made, when, by whom, and why. Near Pueblo sites in Canyon de Chelly, there are naturalistic polychrome paintings that are attributed to a Navajo Indian, Dibe Yazhi. These paintings were made in the 1830's.

Such instances are rare. In most areas, the practice of making rock pictures had died out long before trained investigators entered the field.

BY SUBJECT MATTER

Objects depicted in rock drawings can often be a clue to relative chronology. In some Great Basin sites in California, there are pecked representations of the *atlatl*, the spear thrower that preceded the bow and arrow in this country by many thousands of years. In the Coso Range lying between Death Valley and the Sierra Nevada, there are three narrow basaltic gorges where prehistoric hunters left thousands of drawings connected with the hunting of Bighorn sheep. They show graphically the gradual shift from the spear thrower or *atlatl* to the bow and arrow. There are many representations of the stone-weighted *atlatl* associated with the dimmer and more heavily patinated designs. The figures covered with a moderate coating of desert varnish include a few *atlatls*, hunters holding *atlatls*, and many examples of hunters with bows and arrows. The most recent drawings, with little or no patina, often depict the archer but not *atlatls*.

In another section of the Great Basin several hundred miles to the north (Lovelock Cave, Nevada), this weapon change has been roughly dated. Radiocarbon tests and artifact stratification indicate an occupation

Pecked spear throwers, Little Lake, eastern California. These atlatls *added an extra joint to the arm. The circular shape in the middle of the weapon probably represents a stone weight to give added force to the thrust. Photograph by John Cawley.*

span of nearly 3,000 years. At the lowest level, only *atlatl* fragments have been found. The bow appears here about 500 B.C. and completely supplants the *atlatl* by 1 B.C. The introduction of the bow in the Anasazi region of the Southwest came much later—sometime between A.D. 200 and 400.

With the coming of the white man in the 16th century, the historical period begins and we have an approximate dating guide every time the Indian artist included such subjects as horses, guns, ships, priests, and church buildings on his rock panel.

The best of these is the horse and rider as we know the exact date of many of the early exploring and fur-trapping expeditions into the various Indian regions. The first horses to enter the New World (after the native horses became extinct thousands of years ago) were brought in by Hernando Cortes during the conquest of Mexico in 1519. Later, Coronado on his march to Quivira in 1541 introduced them to the Indians of the Great Plains and it is probable that some of the carved pictures of riders found in the Southwest date from this period.

Juan de Oñate established the colony of New Mexico in 1598, bringing with him horses, cattle, missionaries, and settlers. As trading expeditions went north on both sides of the Rockies, knowledge of the horse traveled

Hunters with atlatls *and mountain sheep, Petroglyph Canyon, Coso Range, California. Photograph by Donald Martin.*

Horsemen and buffalo painted in red, Meyer Springs, Texas. Bullet holes and names have been repainted. Photograph by Dale Ritter.

into the Plains and various tribes began acquiring them (usually by theft) and building up their own herds. The movement of horses from their Spanish point of origin was not a rapid one—the Pawnee on the Central Plains were using horses for hunting early in the 18th century and the Cheyenne to the west had their first horses about 1780. In the Northern Plains, the Blackfeet obtained horses from the Kootenay, Shoshone, and other tribes across the mountains about 1800. When the Lewis and Clark expedition traveled through the Northern Plains in 1803–4, they noted that all tribes seemed supplied with horses. The rock drawings in the Plains region very often show mounted riders; thus none can be dated much before 1750 and most must have been made after 1800. In California, the first horses were brought in by Juan Bautista de Anza in 1775 and there are crude representations of riders in a cave directly above one of his known camp spots in Riverside County. Drawings of horses are rare in southern California and nonexistent in northern California, for with the arrival of the Spanish, the mission system quickly destroyed the major Indian cultures and with them the practice of making rock drawings.

Dated Indian painting in red (left) and black (right) showing animals and a Japanese fishing boat, Kwakiutl Territory, British Columbia. Redrawn from Gutorm Gjessing, 1952.

Cave paintings in southwestern Texas sometimes show mission buildings and priests. These must have been made around 1600, when the Spanish settlements along the Rio Grande were being established.

In the Northwest, the rock carvings along the coast do not show historically datable subjects but paintings occur in the Kwakiutl and Nootka territories that are in the same realistic style as those done by the neighboring Salish tribes and include such subjects as horses, wagons, steam and sailing ships, and coppers. The sailing ships could date from about 1860 to 1900. Coppers, wealth indicators among the Northwest Indians, occur on a rock panel with a Kwakiutl canoe and the date 1921. On the same panel are some animals, a Japanese fishing boat, and the legend SUTSUMA 1927. As the dates are in the same pigments as the rest of the drawing, there is little doubt they are contemporary and unique—a dated Indian painting!

The foregoing dating techniques establish that rock drawings have been made by the American Indian for several thousand years, the practice continuing in certain areas until very recent times. The earliest examples may be in the Great Basin region of eastern California and southern Nevada, with the curvilinear style and the associated *atlatl;* the most recent, the Kwakiutl paintings from British Columbia.

There is at present no evidence that rock paintings or carvings were made during the early millennia of man's wanderings in the New World but someday such evidence may be found.

7 IMPORTANT DESIGN MOTIFS

Red painting, Meyer Springs, Texas. From photographs by Donald Martin.

Though techniques and styles vary tremendously across the country, a number of highly distinctive design elements occur, with local variations, over vast areas. The seven chosen for discussion in this chapter seem of particular interest. The first three—the hand, the bear track, and the thunderbird—are found in almost every major rock drawing area in North America. The others—the mountain sheep, the shield figure, the plumed serpent, and the humped-back flute player—have a more restricted range.

THE HAND

Perhaps the earliest drawings of man are the hand stencils in the caves of southern France and northern Spain. The technique is similar in all these sites—the subject placed his hand flat against the rock wall and the artist blew a diluted pigment around the edge of the hand, giving an effect exactly like modern "air brush" painting. Some of these have been dated in the Upper Paleolithic, possibly 30,000 years ago. Many of these hands show finger amputation and are identical to hands done in the same technique by Australian aborigines. Finger amputation usually connected with mourning ceremonies was practiced by primitive peoples in many parts of the world. It was done by the Tlingit Tsimshian and Haida in the Northwest and by some of the Plains tribes,[1] but the only instances where mutilation is shown in rock painting are from southwest Texas.

In North America the hand is often the principal motif in a rock panel and in a number of cases in the Four Corners region, the blown-stencil

54

technique is employed, identical with the Paleolithic and Australian examples.

Occasionally a wall surface will be literally covered with hundreds of hand prints. There is such a site in the Santa Lucia Mountains of Monterey County, California. The cave wall is smoke-blackened and some 246 hand prints appear in white. The technique seems to have involved coating the hand with paint, pressing it onto the wall and, when dry, scraping away portions of the impression to give a curious skeletal effect. About 15 per cent of the hand prints were of the left hand, reflecting the usual proportion of left-handedness. There are small children's hand prints at the lower levels and adult hands higher up.

There are many hand prints in Buttress Canyon in northeastern Arizona. They were made by pressing the paint-daubed hand against the cave wall, but most have been retouched by brush. The fingers are elongated and, in some cases, zigzag and voluted patterns have been scratched in the palm areas, giving a decorative effect. The hands here are often paired and seem contemporaneous with the many square-shouldered anthropomorphs painted in the cave. In the newly created Canyonlands National Park in southeastern Utah, the "Cave of 200 Hands" shows the elaborations found in the Santa Lucia and the Buttress Canyon sites in conjunction with realistic animal and human figures.

In southern California, small hand prints of adolescents occur with many of the simple diamond and zigzag designs associated with puberty rites. Pecked designs of hands, common through the Southwest and the Great Basin, usually occur singly on panels with masses of other design elements. There is one fine example of realistic incised palm designs done by the Micmacs in Nova Scotia.

The hand prints were probably a form of signature and where great numbers are found together, may have represented some sort of identification with a tribal unit. In certain instances they were made during a ceremony—this is certainly true of the puberty-rite prints.

Red hand painting, northern Arizona. Redrawn from E. W. Haury.

THE BEAR TRACK

The bear was a most important animal to the North American Indian, the living symbol of strength and courage. To kill a bear, especially the formidable grizzly, was a great feat and no higher badge of courage could be gained by a warrior than a necklace of grizzly claws. The grizzly and the more timid black bear are the most widespread of the North American carnivores and played a major part in tribal ritual and mythology.

In California, certain shamans were known as bear doctors. It was believed that the bear doctor could turn himself into a grizzly and in this

Negative hand prints and positive footprints, Canyonlands National Park, Utah. Photograph by Donald Martin.

form he would destroy enemies. The ferocity and tenacity to life of the grizzly appealed to the imagination of the Indians and the power of such shamans was thought to derive directly from the animal. In the Chumash region of southern California, there is a cave high on the side of a brush-covered mountain where 49 bear tracks are carved into the smoke-blackened sandstone. This may well have been the scene of bear-doctor activities. The mass use of bear tracks was unusual, but there is another example of it pecked on the rocks at Lake Pend d'Oreille, Idaho.

The usual way for the Indian artist to draw the bear tracks was to show the paw pad as a single squarish unit with five round toe pads lined up above. But often, especially in the plains, the paw pad is divided by a lateral center line and the toe pads are replaced by long curving claws—unmistakably a grizzly track. This grizzly motif was used by some tribes like the Hopi as a clan symbol.

The bear track often occurs associated with shield figures in the manner of a heraldic device and at Castle Gardens, Wyoming, there is a plains-type engraving of a clothed figure whose garment is covered with bear-track designs.

East of the Mississippi the bear track is usually in association with other animal and bird tracks, the most common being the deer and the turkey. It is likely that these tracks were made in connection with hunting magic—to help assure success in the pursuit of that particular game.

THE PLUMED OR HORNED SERPENT

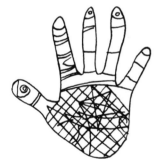

Scratched palm design, Kedgemakooge Lake, Nova Scotia. Redrawn from Garrick Mallery, 1893.

Certain symbols form cultural links between peoples divided by race, religion, and historical background. Such a symbol is the plumed serpent.

The chief deity of the great Toltec civilization of Mexico (A.D. 856–1250) was Quetzalcoatl, god of learning. Legends describe him as a bearded white man who taught the Toltecs the arts, the calendar, writing, and law. Quetzalcoatl is often personified as a feathered rattlesnake and representations of him adorn many ruins of temples. The feathered-serpent cult was carried into the Maya country in Yucatan by the Toltecs where the god was known as Kukulcan. The Aztecs (A.D. 1324–1521) took over the Toltec culture and continued the cult of Quetzalcoatl. In the San Francisco Mountains of central Baja California, there is a spectacular plumed serpent sixteen feet long surrounded by black and red men and six deer. We can only guess that the snake deity in this case was somehow related to hunting magic.

North of Mexico, the symbol appears frequently as a feathered or horned rattlesnake. In the Hopi country, there are rock carvings of both types and they also occur on kiva wall paintings in the ruins of Kuaua near Bernalillo, New Mexico, and at Awatovi on Antelope Mesa, Arizona. The Hopi knew him as Palulukon or Water Serpent, and in Zuñi mythology he was Kolowisi, the Great Horned Serpent, guardian of the springs and streams. Beautiful pecked rock pictures of this deity are plentiful in the Galisteo Basin south of Santa Fe, where there were a number of Tewa pueblos between A.D. 1250 and 1692. To the Tewa, this deity was known as Awanyu. Modern black pottery from San Ildefonso portrays the plumed serpent copied from ancient designs. In southeastern United States, the plumed rattlesnake, drawn in the Mexican style, occurs engraved on stone discs, shell gorgets, and pottery at Spiro, Oklahoma; Moundville, Alabama; and Etowah, Georgia. These finely executed draw-

Bear tracks. 1. Pecked, near Santa Barbara, California. 2. Pecked, northern New Mexico. Redrawn from Polly Schaafsma, 1963. 3. Pecked, North Carolina. Redrawn from J. W. Cambron and S. A. Waters, 1959. 4. Incised, Nebraska. Redrawn from Garrick Mallery, 1893. 5. Pecked, Lake Pend d'Oreille, Idaho. 6. Red painting, British Columbia. Redrawn from Douglas Leechman, 1954.

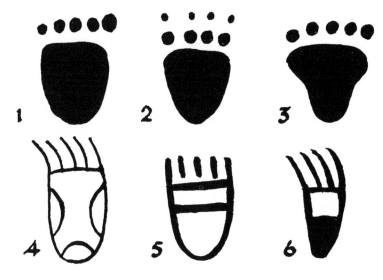

Pecked serpent, Galisteo Basin, New Mexico. Redrawn from E. B. Renaud, 1936.

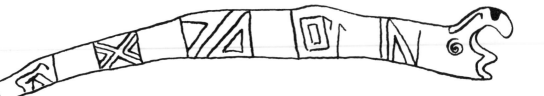

Red painting of tattooed serpent, near El Paso, Texas. Redrawn from A. T. Jackson.

ings are from the Mississippi culture (1200–1600) in Osage and Creek territory. The best examples date from shortly before the coming of the Spanish and indicate strong Mexican influence. Almost nothing is known of what meaning the plumed serpent had for the southeastern Indians. The Natchez considered the serpent second only to the sun symbol in their ceremonies and "tattooed serpent" was the hereditary title of the war chiefs. The Cherokee who overran the Creek territory in eastern Tennessee and northern Georgia shortly before the arrival of the Spaniards called this serpent Uktena and it figures as an evil being in their legends. There can be little doubt that the design but not the cult spread north and east from Mexico not long before the Spanish Conquest.

The northern limit of the plumed serpent in the United States coincides roughly with the northern limit of Mexican influence on cultures and art forms—northern Arizona and New Mexico in the Southwest and southeastern Oklahoma in the Eastern Woodland.

THE THUNDERBIRD

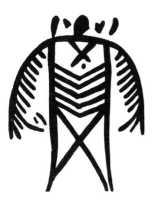

Pecked thunderbird, Alamakee County, Iowa. Redrawn from M. McKusick.

This supernatural being was well known in many areas of North America. Thunderstorms were believed to be caused by an enormous bird that made thunder by flapping its wings and lightning by opening and closing its eyes. The rock drawings of the thunderbird vary from quite naturalistic in the Southwest to highly stylized in the Northwest and Eastern Woodland; but wherever they are found, the bird is always represented with the head to the side and the wings extended in "spread eagle" position.

Some plains tribes believed that the thunderstorm was due to a contest between the thunderbird and a huge rattlesnake or water monster. On the Northwest Coast the thunderbird was supposed to be catching whales during a thunder storm. A Salish tribe in British Columbia thought that the thunderbird used its wings as a great bow to shoot arrows and the noise was caused by the rebound of the wings.

Many tribes used the motif as a clan symbol. With the Hopi, it was the Eagle Clan. The Thunderbird Clan was the most important of the Winnebago Indian clans. This being was their most popular deity and his influence was sought by all. He was a clan ancestor and a guardian spirit bringing success in war and long life. Powerful shamans sometimes claimed to be a reincarnation of this benevolent deity. They pictured the thunderbird on rocks, wood, woven articles, and in effigy mounds.

THE MOUNTAIN SHEEP

The range of the Rocky Mountain sheep and its closely related geographical races covers the mountainous regions of western North America from British Columbia to northern Mexico. Wherever it is found, there are rock drawings of this fine animal.

The mountain sheep is rarely painted, but almost invariably occurs as a pecked design in profile, though sometimes there are attempts to show the head alone front view. Styles range from crude scratched drawings on basalt boulders in southeast Oregon to superb life-sized pecked renderings in the Great Basin region of southeastern California. In the Coso Range of the Mojave Desert in Inyo County, California, are two canyons —known as Petroglyph Canyon and Renegade Canyon—where there are miles of well-executed engraving, including thousands of sheep. Sheep still exist in small bands in these barren mountains and are rigidly protected. These drawings were certainly made for hunting-magic rituals and often hunters are shown with *atlatl* or bow and arrow.

The representations of the sheep are mainly naturalistic but within this limitation, there is a wide range of style. Some have square bodies, occasionally patterned; others have curious boat-shaped bodies, flat on top and round below. The legs are usually shown stiffly vertical but in a few instances there has been an attempt at movement, an innovation doubtless frowned on by the solidly conservative community.

There seems reason to believe that the immense concentration of sheep drawings in this region represents a starting or focal point in the tradition of rendering this animal. Giving some credence to this idea, Robert Heizer and Martin Baumhoff, in *Prehistoric Rock Art of Nevada and Eastern California*, state that analysis of Shoshonean (Uto-Aztecan) dialects of the Great Basin indicates that the ancestral home of the Nevada Shoshoneans (Northern Paiute, Southern Paiute, Western Sho-

Pecked drawing of thunderbird motif, Washington State Park, Missouri. From photograph by Frank Magre.

shonean) is in southeastern California, possibly in the vicinity of Death Valley. The linguistic evidence also suggests the Shoshoneans migrated from this area north along the eastern flank of the Sierra Nevada until they had occupied the entire Great Basin and Colorado Plateau. Besides the tribes already mentioned, this would include the Bannock, Shoshone, and Ute. It has been postulated on the basis of the slight dialect differences over vast areas and on archaeological evidence that this tremendous migration took place between A.D. 1200 and 1800. By the latter date the Shoshonean people were firmly established in their present territories. It would be strange indeed if these peoples did not take their rock-art traditions with them, and the mountain sheep hunting-ritual picture would be a part of these traditions. There are boat-shaped sheep from Monument Valley in southern Utah that are strikingly similar to the boat-shaped sheep from the Coso Range in the California desert.

The sheep (and other game animals) are always rendered in a naturalistic manner even if the rest of the panel is highly stylized and abstract. An unmistakable portrait of the hoped-for quarry was obviously of great importance.

Pecked mountain sheep, Marsh Pass, Arizona. Redrawn from A. V. Kidder and S. J. Guernsey, 1919.

THE HUMPED-BACK FLUTE PLAYER

This engaging and ubiquitous mythical being is found in the Southwest from the Four Corners area into northern Mexico. The portrait of Kokopelli, the humped-back flute player, appears countless times carved and painted on the rocks and painted on the pottery. That he has been a popular figure for a long time is shown by his appearance at Basketmaker sites 1,200 years or more ago. He appears on Hohokam and Mimbres pottery dated at around A.D. 1000–1150 and in association with pottery from northern New Mexico several hundred years later.

The classic type is of a sticklike figure with bent-over back playing on a flutelike instrument (Hohokam red-on-buff pottery). He varies enormously however. Sometimes he leans on a cane, sometimes he holds bow and arrow, often he is outrageously phallic. His hump varies from large to nonexistent. Occasionally he looks quite like a beetle or turtle. In any guise, Kokopelli is unmistakable.

In the upper Rio Grande villages, Kokopelli was said to wander from village to village with a bag of songs on his back, and as a symbol of fertility he was particularly welcome during the corn-planting season. In modern times, certain medicine men in the Andes travel from village to village with a flute and a sack of corn. It is intriguing to speculate on a connection between this modern custom in South America and the humped-back flute player of the Southwest.

Among the Hopi, the humped-back flute player was the symbol of the

Flute Clan. Kokopelli is widely known as a symbol of fertility and used to figure prominently in Hopi dances. God-impersonators dressed with prominent erotic costume-details as Kokopelli and his wife Kokopellimana charmed and delighted the Hopis with their antics but proved too earthy for the tourists. Today, the gay couple appear rarely and in a thoroughly censored routine.

At the Hopi village of Hano, Kokopelli appears as a black man, Nepokwa'i—even the *kachina* doll of this figure is painted black. The Hano people believe the hump is filled with buckskin for making shirts and moccasins to barter for brides. Nepokwa'i may be based on Esteban, the Negro of Fray Marcos de Niza's ill-fated 1539 expedition to find the famed Seven Cities of Cibola. Esteban was stoned to death by the Zuñis for molesting their women.[2] It is not known how far into Mexico this motif occurs but the humped-back creature shown here is from a rock shelter in the Sierra Santa Teressa in Sonora. Nearby was a similar archer shooting an antelope.

THE SHIELD FIGURE

This curious motif is identified with the Rocky Mountain region of the Southwest and Northern Great Plains regions. The northernmost record is from southeastern Alberta, south of Calgary. The major concentrations of the so-called classic shield figure are in Montana, northern Wyoming, and eastern Utah, though it occurs occasionally in southern Idaho, South Dakota, northeastern and central New Mexico, Arizona, northern Texas, and southern Nevada. The most common version consists of a circular shape, usually decorated with heraldiclike partitions and devices. Protruding from this circular design are a head and legs, and often a spear, feathered stick, or lance appears obliquely above the circle at two o'clock or ten o'clock. In other versions, there are one or more arms showing, which hold weapons such a spear, stone club, or bow. Wherever they are found, the drawing technique is the same as the prevailing rock-art technique in the region. In the Great Plains area, the shield figures with rare exceptions are crudely incised on soft sandstone. Occasionally, as at the site south of Calgary and at some Montana and Wyoming sites, the motifs are painted. Many sites in the Colorado drainage of eastern Utah have shield figures—both painted and pecked—that show careful workmanship and ingenious design. In this region the shield figures often occur at sites with the typical Fremont culture petroglyphs. There are a few beautifully painted examples from kiva wall paintings at Kawaika-a and Awatovi ruins, northeast of Flagstaff, Arizona, and at Pottery Mound, near Albuquerque, New Mexico.

Determining where this highly distinctive design motif started is diffi-

Hohokam pottery design of humped-back flute player. Redrawn from H. G. Gladwin, 1937.

Pecked portrait of Kokopelli, the humped-back flute player, Cieneguita, New Mexico. Redrawn from E. B. Renaud, 1936.

cult. Did the idea of the shield figure originate in the Great Plains and spread north and south and west? Or was it part of the Fremont culture pattern of eastern Utah adopted later by nomadic tribes from the plains?

Dating is important here. The oldest sites seem to be in the Fremont area. This culture, apparently derived from the Great Basin, was strongly influenced by Basketmaker and Pueblo traits from the south. It came to an end about A.D. 1150 according to H. M. Wormington. The shield figures from the Fremont area are characterized by lack of arms and the use of geometric designs on the shields. There are no historic period objects like horses depicted at any shield sites.

In the Great Plains area, however, there are a number of sites like those at Writing-on-Stone on the Milk River in southern Alberta, where typical shield figures are shown both with horses and mounted. Identical shield figures on horseback were painted on a Pawnee buffalo robe sometime prior to 1800. Thus, the practice of making shield figures continued well into the historic period. These later shield figures usually have one or more arms to hold various weapons such as the lance, bow and arrow, and war club, and are sometimes phallic. The interior designs on the shield often show animals, animal tracks, and humans.

In Arizona and New Mexico, the motif seems late. The shield paintings at the Awatovi kiva can be dated at not later than 1700 (though they may be at least 100 years older) when the pueblo was destroyed, while those at Kawaika-a are somewhat earlier. The shield figures at Comanche Gap in the Galisteo Basin can be dated at somewhere between 1250, the approximate date of the start of Galisteo Pueblo settlements and 1692, by which time the region was abandoned due to Comanche and Apache attacks. The kiva shield figures are painted while the Galisteo Basin figures are pecked, but in both instances they far surpass in execution and design any other examples of the motif.

The shield-figure motif can scarcely have originated with the Plains Indians. Their history as Plains Indians has been a brief one, dating from the introduction of the horse in the 18th century. Their art was chiefly derived from the Eastern Woodland culture, which never produced anything but the most rudimentary rock-art tradition. Far more plausible is the theory that this singular design motif was created at some time and by someone in the Fremont culture region of eastern Utah; that the motif became popular and spread through this area, ultimately diffusing into distant regions by means of the constant migrations and the forcible displacement of aboriginal populations that was still going on at the beginning of the historic period.

I believe that the earliest shield drawings are associated with warfare between the Fremont people and aggressive nomads from the north—probably the Indians later known as Navajo and Apache. The large shield

Black painting from rock shelter, Sierra Santa Teressa, Sonora.

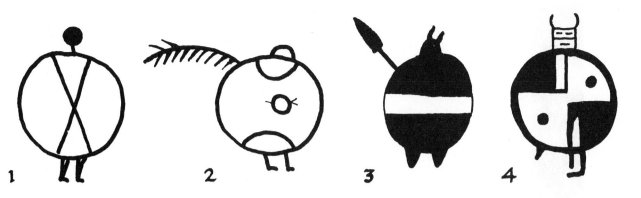

Shield figures. 1. Incised, Writing-on-Stone Park, Alberta. From National Museum of Canada photograph. 2. Incised, Castle Gardens, Wyoming. From photograph by David Gebhard. 3. Red painting, Fergus County, Montana. Redrawn from K. G. Secrist. 4. Pecked, White Canyon, southeastern Utah. Redrawn from Julian H. Steward, 1941.

Detail of Pawnee buffalo robe painting. Redrawn from J. C. Ewers.

Pecked shield figure, Grapevine Canyon, southern Nevada. From photograph by John Cawley.

*Stylized shield figures pecked on basalt,
Galisteo Basin, south of Santa Fe.
Photograph by John Cawley.*

would be ideal for protecting warriors against arrows during an assault on a defended position.

A solid bit of evidence was discovered near Torrey, Utah in 1925—three large buffalo-hide shields decorated in abstract patterns and large enough to cover the entire torso were found in a cave shelter. These shields were radiocarbon-dated just before this book went to press. The tests indicated that they were made between 1650 and 1750 or just prior to the beginning of the horse-oriented Plains culture. The plains warriors developed a small shield averaging about 20 inches in diameter.

The shield drawings in the Fremont area (abandoned by 1150), at Pottery Mound (abandoned by 1450), and in the Galisteo Basin (abandoned by 1692) certainly suggest that the peaceful corn-growers were under considerable pressure from the warlike newcomers.

THE MYSTERY OF THE MINOAN MAZE IN ARIZONA

In the first chapter I stated my belief that the design motifs in North America originated on this continent though there was much diffusion of styles and design elements over vast areas as populations were constantly on the move.

Just south of Oraibi in northeastern Arizona there are five curious symbols in the form of mazes carved on a rock. Near another Hopi town, Shipaulovi, the same intricate design occurs. According to modern Hopi Indians, this design represents the myth of emergence and is called by the Hopis the Mother Earth symbol, Tápu'at (Mother and Child). The passages in the maze are the paths that man must follow on his Road of Life. In southern Arizona, an identical design is carved on the inside wall of the upper story of the ruin of Casa Grande. In 1761 a Spanish traveler in Pimeria Alta (Arizona and Sonora) noted that the Pima drew this symbol in the sand. In his manuscript account he drew a picture of the maze that was exactly like the Hopi versions. A Pima Indian said that the

*Maze design near Hopi town of Shipaulovi,
northern Arizona. Photograph by John Cawley.*

Three examples of Minoan maze. Top—Pecked, Ireland. After photograph in Illustrated London News. *Middle—Maze on silver Cretan coin. Redrawn from H. S. Colton, 1917. Bottom—Pima design, Arizona. Redrawn from H. S. Colton, 1917.*

symbol was used in a children's game and was called the house of Tcuhu. The design is found today in modern Pima basketry.

This symbol is so intricate and so unusual that the idea that it could be independently devised twice is not credible. Yet this maze symbol, *exactly* the same in every detail, occurs in Europe. The earliest example is on an Etruscan vase dating from the late 7th century B.C. Examples are found carved on glacially scratched rocks in the Camonica Valley of the Italian Alps that have been dated between 500 and 250 B.C. A silver coin from Knossos in Crete (200–67 B.C.) features the same maze symbol. A massive block of granite from the Wicklow Mountains in Ireland (the Hollywood Stone) is carved with the identical maze and there are two such designs carved on a ledge in Rocky Valley, Cornwall.

These European mazes appear to be much the same age—several centuries before and after Christ. They are probably Iron Age cult symbols, spreading from Crete through the Etruscan people of northern Italy to the Camunian civilization in the Italian Alps, where culture patterns were affected by the Etruscans to the south and the Celts to the North. The cult symbol might have traveled to Britain and Ireland through the Celtic tribes of mainland Europe or it might have been carried to the islands by the Romans during the Roman occupation, A.D. 43–450.

To explain the appearance of this distinctive symbol in Arizona, Harold S. Colton has listed three possibilities: "First, these symbols may have arisen independently in the new and old world. Secondly, the symbol may have originated in the old world and have been transported to the new in pre-Columbian times. Thirdly that the symbol was introduced into America with the Spanish conquest." [3]

The first possibility can be discarded as a million-to-one shot. Simple basic motifs such as whorls, frets, and crosses will occur to designers anywhere who are working in pottery, basketry, or weaving, but the extraordinary complexity of the Minoan maze would indicate that the design must have spread from a common source. I think the second possibility unlikely as an early introduction would indicate a wider diffusion than the three occurrences in Arizona. It is quite possible that this maze motif in America had a Spanish origin, not earlier than 1600, and that the intriguing design caught the fancy of the Hopi and the Pima.

Carl Schuster, who has been collecting material on this motif for many years, points out the possibility of two additional sites, one in the Galisteo Basin in New Mexico (Tewa Pueblo territory), and the other in the state of Nayarit, Mexico. If this last site could be authenticated, it would greatly extend the range of this extraordinary design in the New World.

There are a number of curious design conventions that appear as details on rock figures. Three of these, the weeping eye, the speech motif, and

Incised drawings, showing heart-line of animal on right, West Virginia. Re-drawn from Garrick Mallery, 1893.

the heart-line, are so distinctive that they can be traced from area to area. Such motifs can be transmitted slowly through exchange of cultural ideas with other tribes and rapidly by migration, where the migrating group take many of their old traditions to their new homeland. Some examples may be the result of independent invention.

The weeping eye (usually vertical lines from the outer edges of the eyes) occurs in the Mississippi culture of southeastern United States, in Wyoming, Montana, Utah, and on the middle Columbia River.

The speech motif (a curved design coming from the mouth of animals, birds, and humans) is found in many Mexican murals and bas-reliefs and in incised shell and copper designs from the Mississippi culture. The only rock-drawing examples are birds with speech symbols in eastern Missouri. This symbol undoubtedly spread north from Mexico in late prehistoric times.

Many Indian tribes drew representations of game animals with a "heart-line" running from the mouth of the animal to the vital organ. The Ojibwa called such drawings *muzzin-ne-neen,* and they were used in hunting-magic ceremonies. When an arrow was drawn piercing the heart of the animal it was hoped that equal success would attend the hunter in the field. This motif is found in West Virginia, Minnesota (where the heart-line also occurs in human figures), Montana, Wyoming, Utah, and New Mexico. It seems likely that this convention originated in the Eastern Woodland and moved through the Great Plains to the Southwest.

8 METHODS OF RECORDING

Pecked bear prints, Lake Pend d'Oreille, Idaho.

The field techniques of recording a rock-drawing site have become somewhat standardized during the last thirty years.

Much of the recording of rock pictures has been by freehand drawing. In many ways it is the poorest method. It takes a rather good artist with a keen and observant eye to copy these paintings and engravings accurately. Unskilled attempts are often worse than useless and bear only the vaguest relation to the original when compared to a good photograph. As a means of copying details too faded or eroded to be picked up by photography, however, field sketches—in pencil or ink, water color or pastels (with approximate scale indicated on the margin)—can be extremely useful. Charles la Monk, a California artist, employed a method of oil paint over a sheet of Masonite sprinkled with eroded sand from the actual rock face to simulate the rock surface. This ingenious technique provides a rather exact facsimile of a small section of painted surface but is entirely too laborious to be considered a standard recording procedure.

Probably the best of the freehand-drawing techniques involves attaching string grids to the rock face with tape. The drawings can then be scaled to the original by making the copy on graph paper or drawing paper with grid drawn to suit desired scale. Different colored inks may be used on tracings of rock drawings to record superimpositions.

Many recordings are made by direct tracings. A common method is to fasten sheets of transparent plastic onto the rock surface with masking tape. The designs are then traced with colored pencils. Henri Lhote, in preparing copies of the Tassili rock paintings in the Sahara, took a team

68

of artists directly to the sites where, armed with great sheets of tracing paper and ladders, they made tracings of all major pictured surfaces. These were then transferred to drawing paper and the finished copies made on the spot. Selwyn Dewdney uses a variation on this technique. He soaks rice paper and applies it to the surface to be recorded with a sponge-rubber roller. The damp paper becomes completely transparent and clings to every irregularity of the rock surface. The incised lines are then traced with a sharpened piece of chalk.

In another method of duplicating carved surfaces, a lightweight cloth (or paper) is taped over the design and a printer's roller carrying oil-base printing ink is rolled over the surface producing a direct-image print.

At sites where the designs are deeply cut, reverse molds may be taken with latex, wax, or plaster of Paris, thus recording even the irregularities of the rock surface. These techniques are used only to record small areas or single figures as the procedure is slow and laborious.

By far the most successful method is photography. It is best to take both black-and-white and color shots of the surfaces to be recorded. The black-and-white shots are needed if the photographs are to illustrate an article or to mount in field books for ready reference. The color slide is indispensable for painted surfaces or where the natural color of the rock is an important factor. In addition, slides can be used for illustrated lectures or classroom work and also for projection on paper if line drawings are required. Most of the text figures in this book were traced from such projections. A good color slide will faithfully give not only the details of the designs but the texture and color of the surrounding rock surface. With the camera, large areas can be covered quickly and accurately.

Most carved and pecked sites can be photographed with available light as they usually occur on cliff faces and isolated boulders, but in many areas the paintings are deep in rock shelters where the creator placed them to escape the weathering effects of wind and water. Here the recorder must often resort to time exposures or flash. The light electronic-flash units available today are very handy for this work and will take up to 150 pictures on one charging of the battery.

When taking picture by available light, the best results are often obtained on a gray day or if the subject is in the shade. Sunlight coming at about a 45-degree angle will sometimes give excellent definition to a carved or pecked design if the surrounding rock is smooth, but if the surface is rough the irregularities can mask the design.

Among rock-art students, there is a sharp difference of opinion on the use of "chalking." One school holds that some designs lack contrast and the only way to get a good photograph is to chalk over the design to heighten the contrast. In the case of some rock carvings where there is no patina to contrast with cut surfaces or where the design has weathered to the same color as the rock mass, there may be some justification for chalking. The dissenters have many objections to it: the original appearance of the drawing is ruined by application of chalk; the work is often done without proper observation, so that different chalkers interpret what they see or think they see quite differently; chalking destroys any effect of superimposition; and with proper illumination, chalking is entirely unnecessary. Use of a side- or top-lighted flash will often bring out details that will not show up on a straight front-lighted subject. Chalk should never be applied to rock paintings since there is no way to remove it without harm to the painting. Pecked or incised rock drawings are usually in exposed positions, and the winter rain can be counted on to wash away the chalk. (I have two publications describing the same rock-pecked panel from the Galisteo Basin in New Mexico; each author had carefully chalked in what he saw or thought he saw on the rock surface and the results were just different enough to allow the two writers to come to startlingly different conclusions.)

Emmanuel Anati, the recorder of the great complex of rock engravings

Pecked drawings (chalked) near Wheeling, West Virginia. String grid is for making scale drawings. Note creature with heart-line in foreground. Photograph from Carnegie Museum, Pittsburgh.

*Author photographing
paintings in the Cara
Pintada Gorge, Sierra
Santa Teressa, Sonora.
Photograph by Dean
Blanchard.*

*Incised drawing being chalked
prior to photography. Milwaukee
Public Museum photograph.*

*Sample form for record-
ing field notes.*

1. SITE   Horse Canyon   2. NUMBER CGK-4   3. COUNTY Kern

4. MAP Bakersfield T32S/R34E/S15   5. ELEVATION   4000

6. LOCATION Driving from Bakersfield, take first canyon road left
   past Monolith. At 3 miles take road Right - drive 2.1 miles -
   cave is high on left across small dry steam. Two caves - painted
   cave to right...27' wide, 6' high, 16' deep.

7. DIMENSIONS OF PAINTED AREA   About 6'x15'

8. KIND OF ROCK   Andesite

9. POSITION OF ROCK   Facing east

10. COLORS   Red,yellow,white,black,green

11. DESIGN ELEMENTS   Abstract 2,4,21,34,37,40,66,67,68 - also a
    number of unique designs featuring curved parallel
    lines to give rainbow effect

12. SUPERIMPOSITION   None

13. EROSION   slight

14. VANDALISM   none

15. ASSOCIATED FEATURES   Many bedrock mortars in adjoining cave

16. REMARKS   Near a heavily traveled road. Possibility of vandalism
    extreme

17. PREVIOUS DESIGNATIONS FOR SITE   none

18. PUBLISHED REFERENCES   none

19. RECORDED BY   Campbell Grant and J. J. Cawley

20. DATE   March 1962   21. PHOTOS   Color

in the Camonica Valley of northern Italy, had a special problem that he
solved in a unique way. The picture rocks were covered with earth and
moss, and when cleaned, had too little contrast to photograph. The entire
design area of the rocks was coated with a thin gouache solution. When
the surface was dry, it was wiped over with a damp cloth, leaving a faint
tint in the incised areas. This method proved far faster and more accurate
than chalking, and the smallest details showed clearly for photography.

It is important to know the scale of the rock pictures and all photographs should include an object of known length, preferably a six- or
twelve-inch ruler.

Often paintings are overlaid with a calcareous deposit from water
seepage, obscuring the designs and making photography difficult. To
overcome this, Henri Lhote in recording the Sahara rock paintings used
an application of kerosene, which made the deposit temporarily trans-

parent. A like result can be obtained with water applied with a small pressure sprayer. In both instances, the reds and blacks are intensified but the paler colors like yellow and white tend to lose contrast.

The field notes should be transferred to a form containing all pertinent information that would enable other students to relocate any recorded site. Such forms are in use by a number of institutions, such as the University of California and the Santa Barbara Museum of Natural History. The general location is marked on a topographical map of the area, which will give elevations, and township, range, and section numbers. Later a sketch map is made to scale, showing pertinent terrain features and boulders or rock faces bearing designs.

9 PRESERVATION OF SITES

White painting near Coyote, Coahuila. Redrawn from J. Alden Mason.

Fifty miles northeast of Santa Barbara, California, are the Carrizo Plains, a forbidding, waterless valley between low desert ranges. Every few years, enough rain falls for the ranchers to mature a scanty wheat crop or to feed cattle. The area is well known to birdwatchers; it is a major wintering spot for sandhill cranes, which come every year by the thousands to feed in the stubble fields. In the center of the plains, an enormous sandstone rock, shaped like a horseshoe, rises over 75 feet, forming a natural amphitheater. On its walls the prehistoric inhabitants of the region painted hundreds of complex polychrome designs (a detail of the main panel, photographed at the turn of the century, is shown here).

Today the site is a complete shambles. Beer cans and empty rifle cartridges litter the ground, and the paintings that survived the gunfire are painted over or carved with names and dates. What was the finest rock-painting site in the United States has been completely ruined by senseless vandalism.

The legacy of aboriginal rock art in the United States is being destroyed at an ever accelerating rate. Before the coming of the whites, the only destructive forces were the natural ones of wind and water. Designs pecked in hard rock are highly resistant to both types of erosion but carvings in soft sandstone and all paintings are highly susceptible to water damage and the scouring effect of wind and wind-blown sand. Only paintings located in favorable spots protected from rain by rock shelters and facing away from prevailing winds have survived with the original brilliance of their color intact.

74

Polychrome painting from the Carrizo Plains, California, as it appeared at the turn of the century. Kern County Land Company photograph, 1894.

Detail of the Carrizo site photographed in 1962, showing the results of vandalism by gunfire.

The immediate and constant danger to these prehistoric drawings comes from the enlightened white man. Some people cannot resist the temptation to scrawl their names over the old Indian designs. Some scratch their name and the date; others use oil paint; the latest method is by paint-spray cans. Another variation of this brainless pattern is to shoot at the rock pictures, anything circular being especially attractive to marksmen.

There is one famous instance in New Mexico where the scribblings of the white man at an aboriginal site have genuine historical interest—at Inscription Rock, El Morro National Monument. This towering landmark, site of two ruined Zuñi villages, has long been a favorite camping spot due to a large natural reservoir of water at the base of the rock. There are hundreds of names incised in the soft sandstone, including that of the first colonizer of New Mexico, Governor Oñate, dated 1605. Many subsequent governors left names and messages alongside those of explorers, soldiers, scouts, traders, and immigrants. A particularly elegant signature is shown here.

But the Sunday beer-can-and-rifle vandal is a minor menace compared with destruction in the name of progress. Topping the list of rock-art destroyers is the hydroelectric and flood-control dam. One of the largest concentrations of aboriginal rock drawings in North America was on the basalt cliffs along the Columbia River from The Dalles to the Grand Coulee. Many large dams have been constructed between these points, taming the mighty river beyond recognition and inundating thousands

An example of handsome vandalism, El Morro National Monument, near Zuni, New Mexico. Photograph by John Cawley.

Pecked drawings near Machiasport, Maine. Site now under water. From Garrick Mallery, 1893.

of rock pictures. When the Glen Canyon region of the Colorado was flooded by the rising waters of Lake Powell, many hundreds of sites were lost. Dams have drowned the West Virginia sites along the Kanawha River and the sites at Safe Harbor on the Susquehanna River in Pennsylvania. Unfortunately aboriginal man, irresistibly attracted to living in the rocky canyons of the great rivers, often made his ceremonial and magical drawings just above high water. With the dams now building and on the drawing boards of the U.S. Army Engineers, a continuing loss of these irreplaceable paintings and carvings can be anticipated. In addition many sites are destroyed each year by road building.

In the last few years, however, the government, though committed to dam construction, has encouraged long-range salvage operations wherever the project threatened extensive archaeological material. Such a salvage operation in the Glen Canyon area is described by Christy Turner in *Petroglyphs of the Glen Canyon Region*. Equally enlightened is the attitude of a few large corporations like the El Paso Natural Gas Company, which has opened up vast areas in archaeologically rich northern New Mexico. Whenever important sites are threatened by road-building or pipe-laying operations, work is held up until the material can be examined and described by experts. The cost of the study and publication costs are met by the company and the projects have come to be known as pipeline archaeology.

The federal government and some state agencies have become increasingly concerned with the destruction of so many of these rock-art sites and a start has been made to save something for future generations. The most successful results have been achieved in the Southwest, where many fine sites are now protected by their inclusion within national parks and monuments, such as Chaco Canyon National Monument, Zion National Park, Canyon de Chelly National Monument, etc. Here trails and roads are created to take the tourists to rock-art sites that are constantly under supervision.

At the state and local levels, a number of excellent attempts to preserve sites have been made. In Massachusetts, Dighton Rock has been moved from its original position, where it was subject to daily inundation by tides, to higher ground. The Ginkgo Petrified Forest Museum at Vantage, Washington, created by the Washington State Parks and Recreation Commission, has on display a number of large blocks of stone covered with rock carvings salvaged before flooding by the Wanapum Dam below Vantage. Farther down the river, the Winquatt Museum at The Dalles has a large collection of such salvaged carved stones. The Arizona State Parks Administration is protecting the Piedras Pintadas near Gila Bend, the site described by Father Kino in 1711.

Many property owners, especially ranchers who have examples of rock art on their property, are very protective, either out of regard for the engravings or paintings themselves or to insure their privacy by keeping the location of such sites secret. The well-known Painted Cave near Santa Barbara has been in private hands for a great many years and the last two owners have maintained a locked iron gate at the entrance. As a result, this fine example of aboriginal art is in good condition, though periodically the lock is smashed and a few names scratched on the painting.

Any and all efforts to save these irreplaceable treasures should be encouraged but much more needs to be done. In the state of California, where the most spectacular North American paintings are found, there is only one rock art site under official protection. This is the vast complex of pecked designs in Renegade and Petroglyph canyons, inside the Naval Ordnance Test Station in the Coso Range of Inyo County. These sites have recently been designated a national landmark and can be visited under Navy supervision.

Part II

ROCK ART AREAS

For convenience in discussing the rock-art zones, I have arbitrarily divided the continent from the Arctic Ocean down to the 23rd parallel in Mexico into nine geographical areas. These areas coincide in the most general sort of way with the natural and cultural regions and rock-drawing stylistic areas. To maintain continuity I have started with the northern section of each rock-art area and worked south.

Most of the rock art in North America occurs on smooth basaltic rock or sandstone, both of which are abundant in or adjacent to the western mountain ranges. In the eastern United States, the majority of the designs are found on the horizontal surfaces of bedrock, usually limestone.

The type of rock to a large extent dictates the technique of applying the drawings. On exposed basalt, sandstone, and limestone, pecking or incising is favored. Both paintings and pecked designs are found on granite. Wherever possible, the paintings are on undersurfaces or areas protected by a rock overhang. The pecked designs are usually cut deeply to bring out patterns, as granite does not give the sharp contrast of patinated basalt or sandstone. In areas where the sandstone forms rock shelters, painting predominates, but in the Southwest, especially in Utah where there are an infinite number of sandstone cliffs covered with dark desert-varnish patina, pecking is the preferred technique.

In areas where ample rock surfaces are present without rock drawings of any kind, the only explanation is that the occupying Indians simply lacked a rock-drawing tradition.

Rock art areas of North America.
1. *Far North*
2. *Northwest*
3. *Columbia-Fraser Plateau*
4. *Great Basin*
5. *California*
6. *Southwest*
7. *Great Plains*
8. *Eastern Woodland*
9. *Northern Woodland*

10 THE FAR NORTH

This forbidding region stretches along the northern edges of the continent from Prince William Sound in Alaska to Labrador in eastern Canada. With the exception of the coniferous forests of the Kodiak Island-Prince William Sound region, it is a land of tundra—wastelands of moss and lichen; a land of bitter cold—short summers and long winters. The Eskimos and the Aleuts sharing a common Eskimo culture live on the coasts of this vast region, seldom venturing far inland.

Modern Eskimos have a rather highly developed art in the form of carved ivory and stone but few of their rock drawings have been recorded. The northernmost site on the continent was found in 1950 by a party of geologists in the foothills of the Brooks Range in northern Alaska. Designs resembling corncobs and deeply incised lines arranged in a rather haphazard manner suggesting tool sharpening occurred on a single sandstone slab. It is quite possible this is doodling by an Eskimo hunting party waiting for game.

Another site in the Brooks Range occurs in a now-empty village that was occupied until the late 19th century, where there are incised boulders in the *kadigi* or men's house. On the Seward Peninsula there are some crude paintings in red and black of human figures. These three sites are the only ones known in northern Alaska.

The next rock drawings are found far to the south on the southwest tip of Kodiak Island—two sites on cliffs and granite boulders at Cape Alitak. The petroglyphs are made by pecking and are from a quarter to three-quarters of an inch in depth. The subjects are human faces of which only the features are drawn, and whales, land animals, and some simple nonrepresentational figures, like spirals and lines of dots. The nonoutlined faces are not unlike those found in the Puget Sound-Strait of Georgia region. Eskimos on Kodiak Island and nearby Afognak Island

Pecked scroll, Wrangell Island, Alaska. From photograph by Edward L. Keithahn.

Eskimo pictographs in red, Prince William Sound, Alaska. Redrawn from Frederica de Laguna, 1956.

81

Pecked mask designs (chalked), Alitak Point, Kodiak Island, Alaska. U. S. Geological Survey photograph.

have reported numerous paintings in red on these islands similar to those on the mainland to the east. According to the Eskimos, the pictures were made for hunting magic and to record game killed.

Frederica de Laguna has recorded many Eskimo paintings in red from Cook Inlet and Prince William Sound, northeast of Kodiak Island. Here again are nonoutlined faces, human figures, game animals, particularly whales and canoes. Eskimo informants said that these pictures were associated with whaling rituals and hunting magic. The nonoutlined face that is first encountered on Kodiak Island is a widespread design motif throughout the Northwest Coast, perhaps the most characteristic of the area.

These Alaskan drawings are all rather crudely conceived and executed. Those from southern Alaska show a strong influence from the Northwest Coast.

The only other Eskimo rock-art site is on the other side of the continent, in northern Quebec. It is located in an old steatite quarry on an island near Wakeham Bay. Saladin d'Anglure, carrying out a social anthropology study in 1961, was taken to the site by Eskimos who were making the trip to get steatite for their carvings. The designs, numbering over 50, were all of masks, some human, others animal. The Eskimos made extensive use of masks, which, among the Chugach and Aleut, were supposed to represent the familiar spirits of shamans. Such masks were worn during ceremonies and are often found with mummies in burial caves. The Eskimo rock drawings appear to be chiefly game animals and ceremonial masks. The masks may represent a cultural trait acquired from the Northwest Coast Indians, who wore elaborate masks in dances to represent supernatural beings. The age of the Eskimo designs is unknown but there are a few clues; they do not appear to have been made by living Indians and there are no articles portrayed of white manufacture. On the other hand, there is no evidence that they are very old. It is possible that most of them are late prehistoric.

Pecked human faces, Kodiak Island, Alaska. After Heizer, 1947.

11 THE NORTHWEST

Along the heavily timbered northwest coast of North America, from Yakutat Bay in southeastern Alaska to Trinidad Bay in California, a unique and complex culture was shared by a number of tribes. The principal groups are the Tlingit, Tsimshian, Haida, Bella Coola, Kwakiutl, Nootka, and Coast Salish. It has often been noted that the higher cultures of America grew out of a settled agricultural economy, but here the leisure time to develop elaborate social and ceremonial patterns was provided by the inexhaustible supply of natural resources along the shores and rivers.

The two major resources of the region were the western red cedar or canoe cedar and the Pacific salmon. Mollusks of all kinds and many large game animals, both land and marine, were important, but it can be said that the culture was essentially a cedar and salmon culture. Although the coastal region had many fine trees like the Douglas fir, the soft, straight-grained cedar was preferred. The magnificent tree gave them canoes, huge communal houses, bark cloth for clothing, and utensils of all kinds, while the immense runs of five species of salmon provided fresh fish for part of the year and smoked salmon for the remainder.

The art forms from the Northwest are widely known and admired; the intricate stylized animal forms that occur everywhere, spectacular totem poles, carved vessels in cedar and argillite, figureheads for the large dugout canoes, and fantastic carved and painted ceremonial masks. It is not surprising that this art tradition dominated their rock carvings too, though with few exceptions their finest work was confined to carving on wood or the easily worked argillite (a slatelike stone without cleavage).

There is no reason to believe that much of the rock art of the Northwest is very old or for that matter that many of their most spectacular achievements, such as the prowed sailing canoe and the gabled communal

Red painting near Tyee, British Columbia. Redrawn from National Museum of Canada photograph.

83

house, with totemic carvings on the front, were not imported ideas. Such canoes and communal houses were long established in Polynesia and a number of writers have remarked on the possibility that these famous voyagers brought new ideas and tools to the Northwest. The totem pole, so characteristic of the Northwest Coast, appears to be a recent development. Many European and American vessels visited the area between 1774 and 1794 and these ships brought iron tools to the Indians. The first totem pole was described in 1791.[1]

From the rock paintings of the Chugach Eskimo of Prince William Sound to the next known examples in southeastern Alaska near Sitka, there is a distance of approximately 450 air miles. Doubtless there are more examples between these points that may be recorded in the future but much of the intervening country is covered with glaciers and heavy forest where inconspicuous rock carvings might well go unnoticed. This is Tlingit territory and the carvings occur on Wrangell and several adjacent islands.

A complex arrangement of figures carved on a boulder near Sitka was interpreted by an elderly Tlingit as a representation of the creation myth. This legend is common to all Northwest Coast tribes and indeed in various forms is found throughout North America.

According to this legend, in the beginning the world was a confused mass of rock and ocean, enveloped in darkness and controlled by powerful spirits who possessed the elements necessary to human life. Yehlh, a benign spirit, who could assume any shape but particularly that of a raven, created man. Over the strenuous objections of the other spirits, he was able to give his children light, fresh water, fire, air, and other good things. After all was done, he disappeared.[2]

On Etoline Island, at about high-tide level, there are many smooth dark rocks, seldom over three feet in diameter, with single figures carved on them. The designs are chiefly animal motifs and represent totemic or clan symbols of the Stikine tribe. There are highly stylized drawings of the wolf, bear, raven, shark, killer whale, eagle, and human head, both outlined and without outline. On Wrangell Island to the east, there are similar carved beach boulders, some with fantastic marine beings referred to by the local Indians as sea monsters.

In the section of British Columbia adjoining Alaska, the Tsimshian territory begins and here all the sites are on the mainland. Several are painted and most of them are on the banks of the Skeena and Nass rivers. Some painted sites feature coppers, the distinctive status symbols discussed in chapter 4 on interpretation. These wealth indicators might have been recorded on stone to commemorate a potlatch or they might have been drawn by someone who hoped to acquire such riches.

South of the Tsimshian territory are numerous carved sites in the terri-

Pecked mythological creatures from Tlingit area, southeastern Alaska. Redrawn from G. T. Emmons.

Stylized head painting with coppers near Tyee, British Columbia. National Museum of Canada photograph.

Pecked sea monster on granite beach boulder (chalked), southeastern Alaska. Photograph by Edward L. Keithahn.

Stylized figures pecked on bedrock, Bella Coola Valley, British Columbia. National Museum of Canada photograph.

tory of the Bella Coola Indians. Here the typical rock picture is deeply incised on isolated boulders. The ubiquitous human face, both outlined and nonoutlined, occurs frequently with anthropomorphs often featuring large eyes and omitting the nose. These are often near river mouths and subject to tidal action and heavy erosion. Drawings in many cases are made on rather small boulders, as in the case of the Wrangell Island carvings.

Farther south are the Kwakiutl, occupying the northwest third of Vancouver Island and adjoining land along the coast to the north. Here there are both painted and carved drawings. The paintings are certainly later than the carvings, some having been made in the last forty years, and show strong influence from the Coast and Inland Salish, with realistic figures quite unlike those in the typical stylized Northwest tradition.

The Coast Salish occupied the circumference of the Gulf of Georgia, Puget Sound, and most of western Washington down to the Chinook territory along the lower Columbia. These people, closely related to the Inland Salish of the Fraser-Columbia Plateau, seem to be late-comers to

Beach boulders with masklike designs, Bella Coola River, British Columbia.
National Museum of Canada photograph.

Fish shapes on boulder, Nanaimo, Vancouver Island. National Museum of Canada photograph.

Pecked drawings of sea monsters, Nanaimo, Vancouver Island. National Museum of Canada photograph.

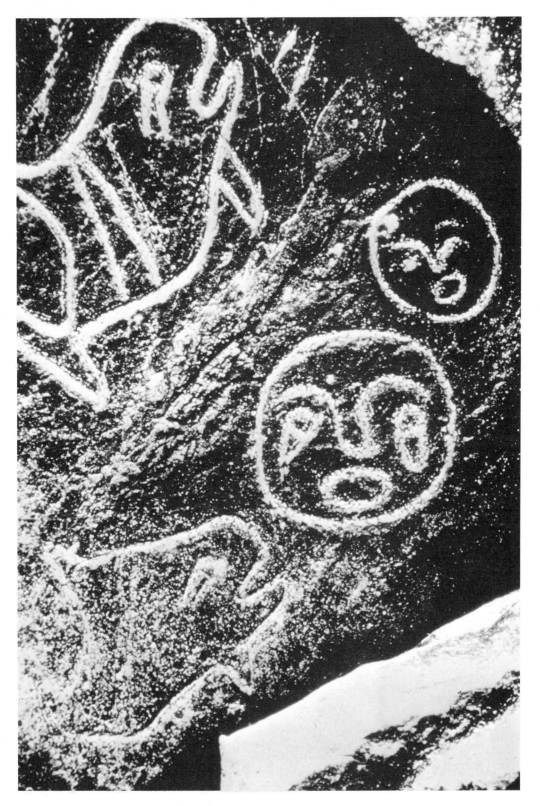

Killer whales and masks pecked on granite (chalked), Cape Alava, Olympic National Park. Note weeping eye. Photograph by Dale Ritter.

Head of Tsagaglalal, mythical woman ruler, pecked on basalt with traces of red paint, near The Dalles Dam, Oregon. Photograph by Jean Hillis.

the coast, having pushed down the Fraser and spilled over the Cascades into western Washington. Many rock-art sites are known from this region, both painted and carved. The carved sites are older than the painted and are in the tradition of the Northwest petroglyphs farther north. At Sproat Lake and at Nanaimo on Vancouver Island, there are outstanding examples of carved mythological beings not unlike the sea monsters from Wrangell Island. On the shores of the Strait of Georgia and in Puget Sound there are carved beach boulders with outlined and nonoutlined heads, like those in the Bella Coola territory and farther north.

The painted sites, almost invariably done in red, are quite naturalistic, featuring canoes, salmon, cetaceans, deer, a double-headed animal with snakelike body, humans, ladderlike designs that might represent salmon weirs, and the classic type of thunderbird. Occasionally painted heads are reminiscent of the carved heads. A good clue to the age lies in the fact that the drawings closely resemble those painted on the power boards used in the great winter ceremony of the Indians around Puget Sound—power boards that were made up until quite recent times. For the most part, the Coast Salish paintings are done in the same manner as those made by the Inland Salish tribes along the Okanogan and Fraser rivers.

The warlike Nootka, who occupied southeastern Vancouver Island, made both painted and carved designs. A number of painted areas in Nootka Sound depict horses and other postcontact motifs, and are in the realistic style of the nearby Coast Salish. South of Puget Sound there are a few carved sites on the lower Columbia that reflect the classic Northwest style. A noteworthy example is the carved and painted head of Tsagaglalal, a legendary woman ruler who was turned to stone by Coyote. It is very skillfully pecked into basaltic rock high above the Columbia River at the present site of The Dalles Dam. Remains of red paint on the rock suggest that the lines of many of the Northwest carvings were originally filled in with paint that has eroded away.

12 THE COLUMBIA-FRASER PLATEAU

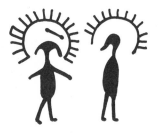

Red painting, Okanogan River, Washington. Redrawn from H. Thomas Cain.

This region embraces the middle Fraser River watershed and the Columbia drainage above The Dalles. In British Columbia, it is mainly a hilly country with many long river and lake valleys enjoying a mild and dry climate. In the United States, the middle Columbia country to the east of the Cascades is hot and dry. Some of the tributaries are very large rivers such as the Deschutes, Salmon, and Snake rivers cutting through deep gorges and semidesert country. Bordering the plateau country are the heavily timbered Cascade Mountains to the west and the Rocky Mountains to the east.

The Inland Salish tribes, closely related to the Coast Salish on the west of the Cascades, occupied a territory from the middle Fraser River, British Columbia, to the Columbia River near Vantage, Washington. There are many rock-art sites and the techniques and styles are remarkably similar over the whole region. The northernmost sites are in Shushwap country above Lillooet. They are mainly carvings on flat rock surfaces and boulders along the Fraser Canyon. A few paintings on limestone are quite realistic, showing men with bows, bighorn sheep, bear paws, salmon, thunderbirds, and a motif that is very often seen to the south in the Columbia drainage—a semicircular shape with attached rays. Additional designs here are canoes, beaver, and cranes. These paintings are all rather crudely done, suggesting the use of the finger as paintbrush, and are in red with occasional black or yellow.

To the east, similar paintings are found in the territory of the Okanogan Indians and include horsemen, additional evidence that most, if not

92

all, of the existing Salish paintings are recent—late prehistoric and historic. Many of the sites are located on cliff faces overlooking the confluence of two streams.

Along the lower Okanogan and upper Columbia rivers in Washington, the paintings become more sophisticated, the execution is more careful, and new design elements are encountered. It is obvious that in this region, brushes of several sizes were used, allowing for better workmanship. The rayed semicircle (sometimes referred to as "sunburst") appears with increasing frequency, sometimes alone but more often forming a halo above single anthropomorphic figures and twinned anthropomorphic forms. The "twinned" brothers is a common motif as far down the Columbia as Vantage and represents characters from a widespread Indian myth. Other new elements include patterns made with a series of dots and animals enclosed in circles.

The Columbia River from the Okanogan to The Dalles had innumerable rock-drawing sites prior to 1941, when the Grand Coulee Dam went into

Red paintings of bear tracks and stylized figures, Pavilion Lake, British Columbia. National Museum of Canada photograph.

Red paintings near Lytton, British Columbia. Redrawn from N. Hallisey.

operation. There are now ten major dams between Grand Coulee and Bonneville dams. Most of the rock-art sites are inundated and we have only drawings and photographs of many of them.

From Wenatchee and on south, rock carvings occur in association with paintings. The subject matter is identical to what has been described on the lower Okanogan and the shift to carving reflects the type of rock available. Through much of the Salish territory, the "country" rock is granite, which is excellent for paint but a poor surface for pecking or incising, while the basalt cliffs of the Columbia Gorge below Wenatchee, with their dark desert-varnish patina, make an ideal surface for pecked petroglyphs.

Drawings of animals, especially the deer and the mountain sheep, are common along the river gorge and there is one site with a good painting of a buffalo. Occasionally the animals are pierced with a spear or arrow. The rayed arc becomes highly elaborate, with double arcs and radiating dots, and the twins appear with horned and feathered headdresses and sometimes as fish. Fish are rare, although this is the great salmon river south of Alaska. The best site on the river was near Vantage, with over 300 figures, but the pictures are all under water today. Near Yakima, the rayed arc becomes a headdress surrounding a nonoutlined face of eyes and nose. This is the most characteristic motif from the middle Fraser River in British Columbia to The Dalles in Washington.

The main travel route along the Columbia was by water and the canoe traffic has been vividly described by Lewis and Clark. The concentrations of rock pictures were at village sites, fishing centers, and trail crossings. The middle Columbia was a meeting ground of cultural influences, from the Great Plains to the east and from the Northwest. The arrow-impaled animals in the gorge are in the tradition of the Plains, where such drawings are plentiful. There are no examples in the middle Columbia of

Red painting, Omak Lake, northeastern Washington. Redrawn from H. Thomas Cain.

Stylized and abstract drawings on the Columbia River near Beverly, Washington. Site is now destroyed. Wenatchee Museum photograph.

Elk and mountain sheep near Vantage, Washington. Wenatchee Museum photograph.

Mountain sheep panel salvaged before flooding by Wanapam Dam, Columbia River, Washington. Now at Ginkgo State Park, Vantage, Washington.

Bear tracks, game animals, an. humans painted in red and blac Salmon River drainage, Idah Photograph by Donald Marti

Caucasian objects or horses; either the drawings predate the coming of the whites or there simply was no contact between the whites and the Indian rock artists.

At Big Eddy above The Dalles Dam, a typical Northwest carving of Tsagaglalal occurs on the same rock face with characteristic middle Columbia rayed arcs painted in red and white. There were famous fishing grounds at the Long Narrows near The Dalles before the building of the dam, and the great river for several miles was compressed to a several-hundred-foot-wide channel of boiling white water. At the fishing camps near the falls and rapids, the Chinook and various Sahaptin tribes carved and painted their designs. Characteristic motifs from this area include the four-pointed star and an owl symbol known locally as the Spedis owl. Mountain sheep drawings are plentiful but again there are few pictures of salmon. It seems certain that the deer and sheep were always drawn in connection with hunting magic to aid in the securing of these wary animals—the easily taken salmon, on the other hand, needed no fishing magic to be brought to the nets or harpoon. In addition, the rock pictures of this region include many strange anthropomorphic beings reminiscent of Northwest mythological creatures.

The rock paintings and carvings on the Columbia tributaries in Idaho bear little resemblance to those in Washington. The sites in northern Idaho are all on or near big lakes. A ledge of schist on Lake Pend d'Oreille is decorated with 28 bear tracks done in the northern plains style and on Lake Coeur d'Alene to the south there is a pecked site with abstract designs. The Salmon River of central Idaho flows through heavily forested country and on granite cliffs and in caves there are many paintings. These are crudely done in red and closely resemble in style and subject the paintings found in western and central Montana. The paintings are representations of humans, large game animals, arrows, tepees, and horsemen—suggesting a strong northern plains influence from the eastern side of the Rockies, and dating many of them as post-1750, when the Indians of the region were beginning to acquire horses.

To the south, the environment and the rock art are very different. The Snake River plain is high sagebrush desert country with the river cutting through the lava bedrock. Rock-pecked designs are found along the lava cliffs—the Indian artists took advantage of the patina-blackened rocks and paintings become rare. The designs from this area differ greatly from the paintings of central Idaho. They are stylized and abstract in typical Great Basin style, though occasionally Plains motifs occur, like the curved-claw bear tracks and shield figures near Gooding. The Great Basin elements are mainly in the rectilinear abstract style and include grids, concentric circles and arcs, dot patterns, triangles, stylized humans, and realistic mountain sheep with horns drawn in front view. The Shoshone Indians, holding the southern watershed of the Snake, were in close contact with the Great Basin and undoubtedly migrated north from that area taking their rock-pecking technique with them.

The principal tributaries of the Columbia in Oregon east of the Cascades are the Deschutes and the John Day, and there are many red-painted sites along both streams. The style is naturalistic with some abstract or indeterminate elements, and is reminiscent of the paintings in central Idaho. Subject matter includes humans, snakes, mountain sheep, deer, hands, zigzags, and rayed circles. The execution of the paintings is quite poor and suggests that the paint was applied by finger. This region was occupied by various Sahaptin people like the Tenino and the John Day tribes.

13 THE GREAT BASIN

Pecked animal, Coso Range, California. From photograph by Donald Martin.

As the name implies, the Great Basin is a vast region with no outlets to either ocean—all the streams empty into marshy sinks or saline desert lakes like the Great Salt Lake in Utah and Mono Lake in California. The Basin includes most of Nevada and sizable sections of Oregon, Utah, and California.

Bounded on the west by the Cascades, the Sierra Nevada, and the California coastal ranges, and on the east by the Wasatch Mountains of Utah, much of the Basin is true desert, with intermittent streams and springs the only source of water.

Unsurprisingly in such a harsh environment the cultural level of the Indians was extremely low. These were the Indians the early trappers and explorers saw grubbing for roots with digging sticks and hence dubbed "Diggers." Zenas Leonard, a fur trapper with the Walker expedition of 1833, describes the Indians (probably Paiutes) he saw near Humboldt Lake:

These Indians are totally naked—both male and female—with the exception of a shield of grass which they wear around their loins. They are generally small and weak, and some of them are very hairy. They subsist upon grass-seed, frogs, fish, etc. . . . Their habitations are formed of a round hole dug in the ground, over which sticks are placed, giving it the shape of a potato hole—this is covered with grass and earth—the door on one side and the fire at the other. They cook in a pot made of stiff mud which they lay on the fire and burn; but from the sandy nature of the mud, after cooking a few times, it falls to pieces. . . .[1]

The culture of the Great Basin Indians is an excellent example of the effects of environment and lack of contact with higher cultures. Most of the Basin people are of the Shoshonean branch of the Uto-Aztecan language family, the same people that in more favorable environments produced the Hopi and the Aztec cultures. The Shoshoneans who migrated northeastward looking for greener pastures acquired the horse and a Plains culture.

The nomadic existence forced on the Great Basin Indians, constantly moving from camp to camp in small hunting and food-gathering bands, precluded the establishment of elaborate ceremonies such as those created by the corn-growing Hopi. It is not surprising that most of the Great Basin rock pictures are very simple and in many instances rather crudely done. What ceremonies existed were doubtless simple rites connected with hunting magic, rainmaking, and fertility.

The rock art of the Klamath and Modoc Indians in southern Oregon and northern California is so typical of the Great Basin that it has been included in this section though that area drains into the Pacific Ocean and the cultures of these Indians are more closely tied to California and the Northwest. Many of the designs are crudely scratched on basaltic boulders; others are painted where slanting rocks afforded some weather protection. The designs are of the simplest type—concentric circles, meandering lines, zigzags, stick men occasionally phallic, elk, deer, sheep, and lizards.

The only site I know where there are paintings in a true cave is near Tule Lake. The entrance is a hole in the ground near tumbled masses of lava rocks, and it was necessary to enter the cave with a rope because of

Concentric circles pecked on basalt with traces of red paint, near Bly, southern Oregon.

Polychrome designs inside a lava tube, Lava Beds National Monument, northeastern California. University of California photograph.

Figures pecked on basalt, Petroglyph Canyon, Coso Range, California. Photograph by Donald Martin.

Mountain sheep, nearly life size, Petroglyph Canyon, Coso Range, California. Photograph by Donald Martin.

Abstract pecked designs (chalked), west-central Nevada. University of California Archaeological Survey photograph.

a 12-foot drop to the ground inside. The cave is a lava tube formed during ancient volcanic action, several hundred feet long and about 30 feet in diameter. Many paintings in black, white, and red occur in the areas free from water seepage.

In Nevada the majority of the many recorded sites are concentrated in the Sierra foothills and near springs and desert lakes. This is the country of the Northern Paiute and the Western Shoshone and there is little doubt that many of the pictures were pecked, painted, or scratched by these Shoshonean people.

Through most of this country the pecked drawings are of the crudest type with meanders, connected circles, grids, and concentric circles predominating, but in southern Nevada and southeastern California something new appears. The sheep that occurred in crude scratched drawings near the Oregon border appear here by the thousands in pecked form and often very well done. Hunters are shown using the *atlatl* as well as the bow, and a few sites depict horsemen, indicating a very long time-span for the rock-art tradition of the region. There are frequent stylized anthropomorphs wearing figured garments and many designs suggesting fabric and basketry motifs. The great numbers of sheep drawings indicate that hunting magic was the basic reason for the rock art of the region. The greatest concentrations are in the California desert regions from Death Valley west to the lower Sierra Nevada. There are some paintings in the desert ranges here, chiefly of naturalistic game animals, but geometric patterns also occur, particularly in the Joshua Tree National Monument.

Red painting, Joshua Tree National Monument, California.

The southeastern California and southern Nevada region is all Shoshonean territory and the principal tribes are the Western Shoshone, Chemehuevi, and Serrano. The tremendous numbers of rock pictures concentrated in the area suggest that the tradition of rock drawing there was a very long one. As noted earlier in chapter 7, this small area might have been the starting point of the widespread Shoshonean migrations that went west, north, and east in search of a better life, taking with them their rock-drawing tradition.

Studies are only just beginning on the rock drawings of western Utah but from evidence at hand, the drawings are in the typical Great Basin styles with Basketmaker and Puebloid influences at the eastern edge, where anthropomorphs with triangular bodies, *kachina* figures, and humans with Pueblo-type side-locked hair occur. This same type of subject is found at many painted sites in southeastern Nevada.

Robert F. Heizer and Martin A. Baumhoff have described seven styles from Nevada: [2]

Style	*Method*	*Characteristic Elements*
Great Basin Representational	Pecking	Mountain sheep, quadruped, foot, hand, horned human, *kachina*
Great Basin Curvilinear Abstract	Pecking	Circle, concentric circles, chain of circles, sun disc, curvilinear meander, star, snake
Great Basin Rectilinear Abstract	Pecking	Dots, grids, rakes, cross-hatching
Great Basin Painted	Painting	Circles, parallel lines
Great Basin Scratched	Scratching	Sun disc, parallel lines, cross-hatching
Puebloan Painted	Painting	*Kachina*
Pit and Groove	Pecking	Pits and grooves

14 CALIFORNIA

Brown and white painting,
Tulare County, California.

California is an extraordinary state—it offers every type of climate and environment. The Great Valley, actually two valleys, the Sacramento and the San Joaquin, is bounded on the west by the coastal ranges and on the east by the Sierra Nevada. To the north is the Cascade Range, and to the south the Tehachapi Range separates the Great Valley from southern California. The rainy northern coast, home of the giant redwoods, extends as far south as Monterey. Below Monterey, the coast ranges become progressively drier until they are semidesert in southern California. Northeastern and southeastern California are included in the Great Basin section.

Of the six language families in America north of Mexico, all but the Eskimo occur in California. In no other part of the country is there anything like this diversity of peoples in so small an area. In contrast, the Algonquian-speaking tribes are found in unbroken sequence from Puget Sound to Nova Scotia. A possible explanation is that California west of the Sierra was on a migration route from the earliest times and groups were continually splitting up as they passed through this region, some liking what they saw and settling there, others continuing onward. With this diversity of topography and peoples, it is not surprising that almost every type of rock art is found in the state.

The rock-art sites in northern California are chiefly of the pit-and-groove type. Almost invariably they occur on isolated boulders in the foothills of the coast ranges and the Sierra Nevada. Ethnographic information indicates that these were used in rainmaking and fertility ceremonies (see chapter 4). In central and southern California, the pit-and-groove style is often found on large outcroppings of granite and in caves. Occasionally the pits are arranged in lines, but the usual method is a random scattering of the depressions on the rock surface. Of all the examples of Indian markings on rock, this type has the least claim to be classified as art. It seems to be a very early variety of aboriginal rock inscription and is found almost everywhere in the world.

North of San Francisco paintings are extremely rare and these are of the crudest finger-daubed type, but numerous pecked and incised designs have been recorded. These are very simple: concentric circles, rakes, bear tracks, and bird tracks. Often the carvings are hidden by heavy lichen growths, and in a number of instances students have had to remove the growth with chemicals or a wire brush before the design could be copied.

The Great Basin pecked technique did not penetrate far west of the Sierra passes, undoubtedly due to the unsuitability of the rock surfaces. The shallow pecking through desert varnish on basaltic rock that produced the striking designs in the Great Basin gave way to deeply pecked and incised designs on the granite and sandstone of interior California.

In the pine and madrone forests of Monterey County are a number of painted sites in sandstone caves, where smoke-blackened walls have been covered with hundreds of hand impressions in white. Many small caves in the nearby canyons have small painted stick figures in red, and diamonds, circles, and grids and ladders done with a piece of charcoal or lump of dark mineral.

The territory of the Chumash Indians, creators of the finest rock paintings in North America, begins at Morro Bay. These Indians, first described by Juan Rodriguez Cabrillo in 1542, were concentrated along the Santa Barbara Channel but their territory extended through the coastal ranges to the San Joaquin Valley, an area roughly the size of Maryland. The Spanish explorers found them superior to the other California Indians they had encountered and greatly admired their artifacts of stone, wood, shell, and basketry. They especially noted in their journals the beautiful sewn plank canoes in which the natives made long ocean voyages.

The Chumash paintings were done in as many as six colors though the usual range was red, black, and white, with many of the sites in red alone. The basic styles are abstract linear and abstract polychrome. With both styles, bizarre and striking anthropomorphic and zoomorphic beings occur with an endless variety of purely abstract shapes. A constantly recurring theme is the circle, with every conceivable variation of spokes, rays, cogs, and curious appendages. The abstract polychrome paintings often have circular designs with multiple outlines of contrasting colors to give a basically simple shape great richness. In almost all instances, the craftsmanship is excellent.

The coastal ranges inhabited by the Chumash are made up of ancient sedimentary rocks and most of the sites are located in shallow, wind-

Red and white painting, mountains of northern Ventura County, California.

sculptured sandstone caves or rock shelters. I know of few pursuits more gratifying than the search for unknown or unrecorded rock-art sites. For example I remember a day spent trying to relocate a painting seen many years before by a deer hunter in the rugged San Rafael Mountains behind Santa Barbara. The trails he remembered had long since disappeared and we traveled with back packs down brush-choked ravines. With endless stops to chop brush with a machete, it was late in the day when we dropped into the main canyon and nearly dark when we found the cave, and entered through a narrow slit in the cliff face. The colors were as fresh as if applied the day before and yet they were painted at least 200 years ago. It is my belief that the paintings in the Chumash area are not very old, based on the lack of superimposition of styles, on the known rate of paint erosion at some unprotected sites, and on the association of datable artifacts with painted caves. The evidence indicates they were done in the last 1,000 years, with some dating from late prehistoric or even mission times.

The most elaborate paintings are found in the innermost mountain

Detail of a panel of more than two hundred hands painted on smoke-blackened wall, Church Creek, Monterey County, California.

The Painted Cave near Santa Barbara, California. This site has been protected with an iron grille and is the best preserved of the California paintings accessible to the public. Anderson Photo Service.

ranges and close to the western edge of the San Joaquin Valley. Farthest removed from this area are the crude red paintings of parallel lines at two sites on the Channel Islands, nearly 30 miles offshore. These islands supported a large population with a somewhat less elaborate culture than their onshore cousins. The implication is that the tradition came to the Chumash through neighboring tribes to the northeast where polychrome painting was done by the Yokuts. As there is nothing in that direction to compare to the finest Chumash paintings, it is reasonable to assume that the Chumash, like many other adaptable peoples, took over a basic idea and mightily improved on it.

Most of the Chumash paintings are unvandalized, thanks to their location in extremely rough brush-covered mountain country, where their

Polychrome panel at Carrizo Plains, California, as it appeared in 1894. The painted area was more than one hundred feet long. Site has since been destroyed by vandals. Kern County Land Company photograph.

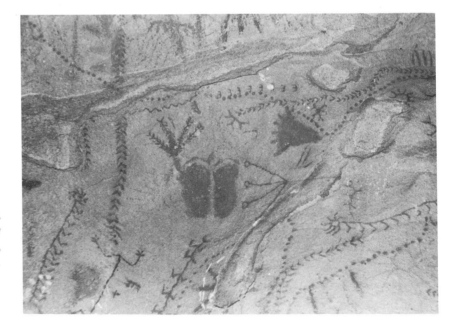

Red Chumash painting, San Rafael Range, Santa Barbara County, California.

existence was largely unknown until a survey made in 1961-63. The examples in open country or near public roads have been destroyed.

San Nicolás Island, 60 miles off the southern California coast, was inhabited by Shoshonean-speaking Indians sharing many cultural traits with the Chumash. There are incised drawings of porpoises and killer whales on the walls of a sea cave, indicating the importance of these large marine mammals in the life of the people.

Across the San Joaquin Valley lived the Yokuts, an Indian nation that was divided into about 40 tribes. It was the largest ethnic group in California before their deliberate decimation by the land-hungry settlers. Much of the valley was marshland fed by the Kern and King rivers, which formed large shallow lakes. Around these lakes and along the creeks in the foothills of the Sierra Nevada, the Yokuts lived in much the same manner as the Chumash. There was much trade between the two peoples and it is not surprising to find a great similarity in their paintings. The design motifs, especially the abstractions, are different but the technique is very much the same. At a few of the sites near Porterville and Exeter, the execution of the paintings is carefully done and considerable imagination is shown in the designs. There is only one example of animals drawn in a side view in Chumash territory (four mounted horsemen at a site on the extreme eastern boundary) but the occurrence of this style (as opposed to the spread-eagle or pelt convention) is frequent along the Sierra foothills in the rendering of deer, coyotes, cattle, and horses. The excellent condition of many of the Yokuts paintings and the occasional drawing of horsemen would indicate that many of them are late prehistoric and historic.

Adjoining the Yokuts territory to the southeast are the Shoshonean Tubatulabal of the Kern River and the Shoshonean Kawaiisu of the Tehachapi Mountains. Both of these peoples sporadically occupied country on the Great Basin side of the Sierra divide but their drawings rather closely follow the Yokuts design style and technique. A certain number of the pictures are polychrome in red, black, and white, but most are limited to red.

The last region with large concentrations of rock drawings is in southwestern California. With few exceptions they are paintings and are quite different from those in any other section of the state.

South of the Chumash territory were the Juaneño and Luiseño, Shoshonean tribes who shared ceremonial practices with the Chumash, including the ritual use of the narcotic jimsonweed. It has been suggested that many of the paintings were made while under narcotic influence. The Juaneño revered the condor as sacred and the great bird figured prominently in their ceremonies. In the Luiseño territory south of Riverside are numerous drawings on granite boulders and outcroppings featur-

Red, white, and black painting, Caliente Range, California.

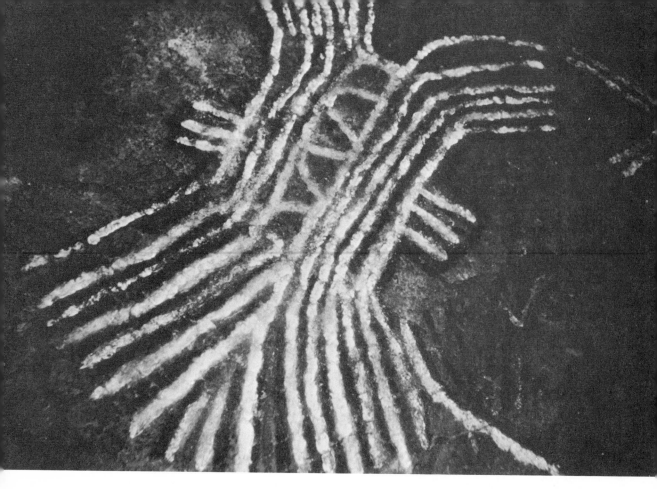

Yokuts painting in red, black, and white, Tulare County, California.

Maze pecked on granite near Hemet, California. This may not be of Indian origin as there is nothing like it in style or technique in the region.

ing red linear designs of diamonds, zigzags, parallel lines, hand prints, and cross-hatching. These were all made during puberty rites (see chapter 4).

Near Hemet, a handsome square maze design, quite unlike anything else in the region, is pecked on a granite boulder. Sixty miles to the south are somewhat similar designs in the Diegueño area, but these are all painted and are fret designs and not true mazes. There is a strong probability that this striking design has a non-Indian origin.

The areas just described were occupied by Shoshonean groups that had migrated to the west coast from the Great Basin and their rock paintings can all be described as rectilinear abstract. It seems probable that the southwestern California paintings derived from the Great Basin rectilinear abstract (pecked) and the Great Basin painted.

Near the southern border of the state are the Diegueño Indians, members of the scattered Hokan-language family that included the Chumash. These Indians were the first to come under the mission system in upper California and survived the ordeal remarkably well. Alfred Kroeber estimated their numbers in 1775 at about 3,000. Today there are over 500. Their survival must be attributed to their strong spirit of independence and resistance to the missionaries.

Elaborate fret and mazelike painting in red, Green Valley near Poway, southeastern California. These paintings are nearly eroded away and cannot be very old. San Diego Museum of Man photograph.

The only major concentration of paintings in the Diegueño territory is in Green Valley near Poway. The style is rectilinear abstract, like the basic style in the rest of southwestern California, but the design motifs are extraordinary. There are many variations on geometric fret patterns, and in some instances very large rock surfaces are entirely covered with an integrated pattern. Unfortunately the paintings, invariably in red, are on exposed granite surfaces with no protection from the elements and are rapidly eroding away. In addition, suburbia has discovered Green Valley and bulldozers are assuring the speedy and total destruction of these interesting paintings. There are a few examples in the valley of typically Great Basin style pecked designs—dotted patterns and curvilinear meanders and circles.

The Sierra Nevada of California between the San Joaquin Valley and the Great Basin sharply separates the two basic rock-drawing techniques. East of the barrier, rock pecking is overwhelmingly dominant; west of the divide, most of the drawings are painted. An equally abrupt cleavage exists between the northern and southern halves of the state. North of the San Joaquin Valley, the designs are mainly pecked and incised; south of the valley they are painted.

Red painting, Riverside County, California.

MAIN CALIFORNIA ROCK-DRAWING STYLES

Style	Method	Major Concentration
Abstract Linear	Painted	Southwestern California
Abstract Polychrome	Painted	Coastal ranges (Santa Barbara area) —Sierra foothills (Kern-Tulare counties)
Abstract Curvilinear	Pecked-Incised	Northern California
Pit and Groove	Pecked	Northern California

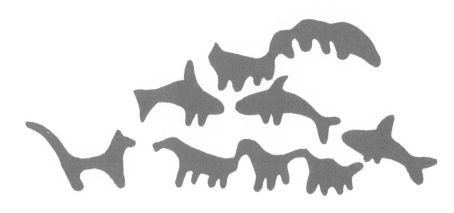

Killer whales and other animals painted on granite, Cook Inlet, Alaska. Redrawn from Frederica de Laguna, 1933. Total width sixteen inches.

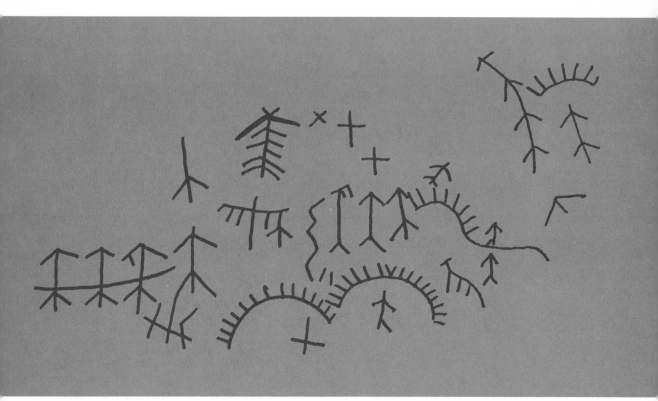

Puberty ceremonial painting on granite, Thompson River, British Columbia. Redrawn from James A. Teit, 1896. Width is five and one-half inches.

Paintings on granite, Tramping Lake, northern Manitoba. The open-mouthed buffalo are unusual. Elements slightly compressed. From photograph by Tim Jones. Left buffalo is twenty inches long.

Thunderbird and ceremonial figure, possibly bear doctor, painted on granite, Medicine Rapids, Saskatchewan. From photograph by Tim Jones. Height of panel is about four feet.

Elk, mountain sheep, and other game animals painted on granite, Salmon River, central Idaho. From photograph by Donald Martin.

Geometric design on granite boulder near Poway, California. From San Diego Museum of Man photograph. About four feet square.

Chumash painting on sandstone. Part of a very large series of designs, San Luis Obispo County, California. Width of pictured section, three feet.

Luiseño puberty rites painting, Riverside County, California. Panel is four feet wide.

Chumash painting from a sandstone shelter, San Rafael range, southwestern California.
Only the Chumash and the neighboring Yokuts painted on smoke-blackened surfaces.
Width of panel is three feet.

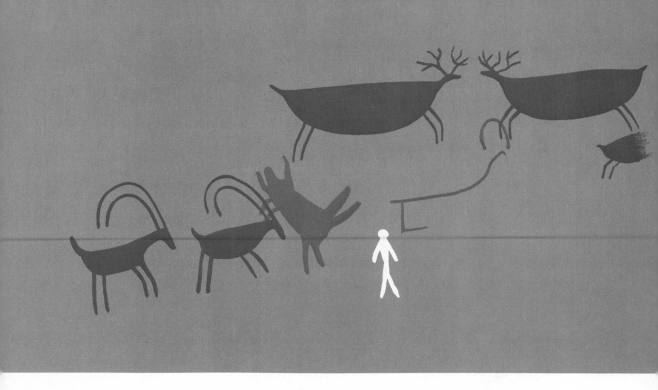

Deer and mountain sheep painted on granite, Coso Range, Inyo County, California. The deer at right is sixteen inches long.

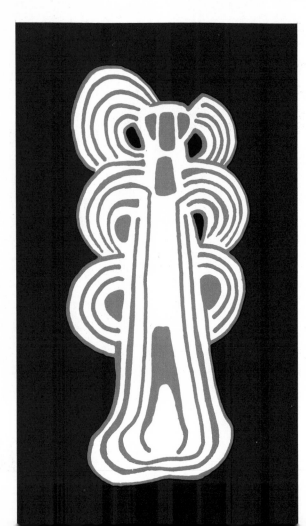

Yokuts ceremonial designs painted on granite near Exeter, California. Length about ten feet.

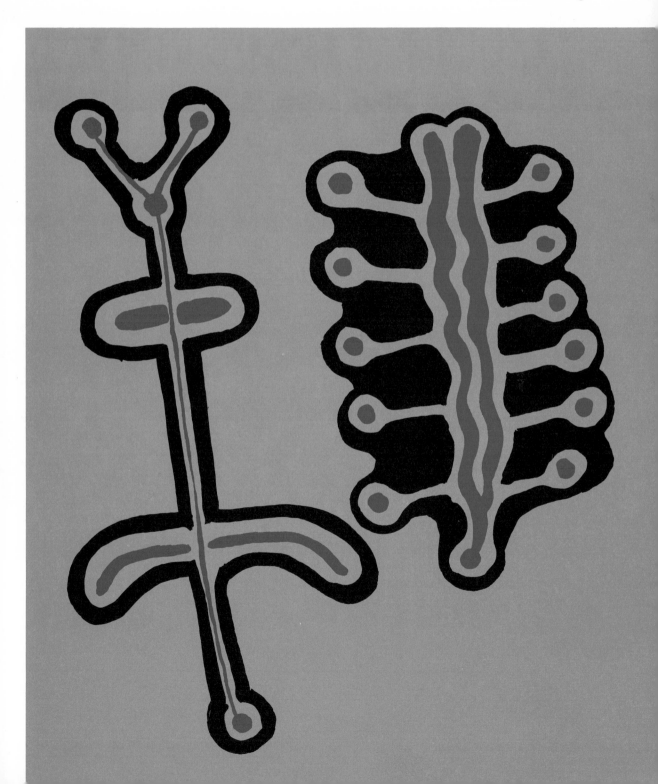

Detail from large Yokuts ceremonial designs painted on granite, Tule River Indian reservation, Tulare County, California. Design on left is sixteen inches long.

Painting at Rocky Hill, Tulare County, California.
Length of panel six and one-half feet.

*Painting on sandstone cliff, Parunuweap
Canyon, Zion National Park, Utah.
From photograph by Ben Weatherill.
Height seventeen inches.*

Elaborate painting on sandstone near San Ygnacio, central Baja California. The main figure, a plumed serpent, is apparently surrounded by worshipers. From photograph by Velma Pontoni. Panel is nineteen feet long.

Supernatural figures painted on sandstone cliff, Barrier Canyon, eastern Utah. From photograph by Donald Martin. Width of panel fourteen feet.

Navajo painting on sandstone of Spanish horsemen, Canyon de Chelly, northern Arizona. (Early 19th century.) From photograph by J. J. Cawley, Approximately one-half life size.

Navajo ceremonial painting from Delgadito Canyon, northwestern New Mexico. This can be dated as 18th century when the Navajos in the area were strongly influenced by Pueblo culture. The left figure is one foot high.

Part of a large painting on a limestone rock shelter, Terrell County, Texas. Elements such as priests and horsemen date this panel after the arrival of the Spaniards. It was probably the work of Apache Indians. From photograph by Donald E. Martin. Length of pictured section is seventeen feet.

Polychrome panel featuring thunderbird and antelope with heart-line, attributed to the Mescalero Apache. Located in the Sierra Blanco, near Ruidoso, New Mexico. The panel is about five feet long.

Stylized human figures on rhyolite near Hermosillo, Sonora, Mexico. Pictured section is about twenty-six inches wide.

Painting on sandstone cliff, Ralls County, Missouri. Drawings showing action are rare in North America. From photograph by Frank Magre. Figures are ten and one-half inches high.

Headless figure connected with "power" line to unidentified symbol is Michigan's only rock painting. It is located near Manistique, in what was Menomini territory. From Mackinac Island State Park photograph.

15 THE SOUTHWEST

The Southwest as defined in this study is divided into two almost equal parts by the U.S.–Mexican border. It includes the drainage areas of the Colorado and Rio Grande rivers, the southern Rockies, the Sierra Madre of Mexico, and the peninsula of Baja California. The Colorado and its tributaries have cut immense canyons through the Colorado Plateau. Particularly spectacular are the red sandstone cliffs in eastern Utah, which have attracted Indian artists for countless generations. This is a country of juniper, piñon, and sagebrush, with pines in the mountains. In Arizona, the Mogollon Rim drops off to the south and true desert conditions extend into much of Sonora and Chihuahua, where the creosote bush and cactus are characteristic plants.

A very distinctive type of rock picture is found in eastern Utah and western Colorado. Large human figures, sometimes over-life-sized, are pecked on the smooth sandstone cliffs. They are almost invariably front-faced with highly elaborate headdresses, earrings, necklaces, and belts. Often the eyes are drawn with vertical lines below them, a widespread convention known as the "weeping eye." Occasionally a figure has lines filled in with color; in rare instances the entire figure is painted.

Near Vernal, Utah, is a canyon with many beautifully carved figures of this type. The panel shown on page 117 is over 75 feet from the ground and may be the finest example of aboriginal rock-carving in the United States. A number of the ceremonial figures are depicted with shields, while others carry long-necked heads which may represent masks or trophy heads.

These designs are typical of the Fremont culture, first discovered at the Fremont River in southern Utah. Sharing many traits with the Anasazi (Basketmaker-Pueblo), including corn agriculture, this culture was wide-

White painting, Cave Valley, Zion National Park, Utah. From photograph by Ron Wauer.

115

Ceremonial figures pecked on sandstone cliffs (chalked), Dry Fork Canyon, near Vernal, Utah. Photograph by Dale Ritter.

spread in eastern Utah and western Colorado until about 1150. What happened to these people is unknown but a good possibility is that they were overwhelmed or displaced by the Shoshoneans pushing in from the Great Basin to the west and by Navajos migrating down from the Northern Plains. The Fremont people might have moved south to live with the Anasazi of the Four Corners area, where Utah, Colorado, Arizona, and New Mexico meet.

There are many examples of both painted and pecked shield figures in the Fremont area (see chapter 7). Occasionally they occur in association with the large, highly decorated ceremonial figures but are not necessarily of the same age or culture.

In southeastern Utah near the confluence of the Green and Colorado rivers there are a number of very unusual painted sites. The typical motif is a mummylike anthropomorphic figure without arms or legs and often without features. These figures range from several feet to well over life-size. The paintings are in various shades of red-brown and the larger figures have intricate fabriclike designs incised through the paint or added in white. They are in the Fremont area but are quite unlike the typical examples. This must have been a local development that had little or no influence on the surrounding regions. A few examples of this style are known in pecked form.

In southeastern Utah, there are vast numbers of pecked designs; often a single rock surface will be covered with motifs in a completely disorganized manner—mountain sheep, animal tracks, curvilinear meanders, etc. A well-known site of this type is in the Petrified Forest National Park in Arizona and others are in the Valley of Fire of southern Nevada. The style at these sites shows a strong Great Basin influence, not surprisingly, since during this period so many people were on the move.

Near Moab, in association with mountain sheep, there is a pecked rendering of what is locally known as the "mastodon" and widely believed to be a life portrait of that extinct beast. It is a three-toed trunked animal but the brightness of the design and its lack of patina, together with the fact that the adjoining mountain sheep and accompanying initials have some patina and so are older, brand it a hoax. The last mastodons died out about 6,000 years ago.

The western Colorado sites that have been described indicate a meeting

Life-sized figures pecked on sandstone, Dry Fork Canyon, near Vernal, Utah. Traces of red paint appear on the shield of the central figure. Photograph by Donald Martin.

of the Fremont pecked-drawing tradition with a late Plains influence. The horse never occurs in the Fremont drawings but is present at several Colorado painted sites.

In the Four Corners region, there are a great many rock drawings reflecting the very long occupation of the country by an agricultural people with ample time to develop elaborate ceremonies connected primarily with the growing of corn. The Anasazi, a peaceful, industrious people, developed the highest culture north of Middle America. Along the Glen Canyon section of the Colorado River and the San Juan, a major tributary, the earliest pictures are from the Basketmaker period (pre-A.D. 800) and are usually painted, though pecked designs have also been assigned to this period. Square and triangular-bodied anthropomorphs with small heads are common but the most abundant pecked design is the mountain sheep. The rock drawings in the Four Corners are often closely associated with spectacular ruined cliff dwellings, built into the sides of enormous sandstone cliffs. Happily the finest of these canyon ruins are rigidly protected by the government. Many of the rock drawings of this area, and indeed of the entire Colorado Plateau, strongly suggest the Great Basin and may be the work of the nonagricultural Shoshonean Utes.

During the Pueblo period, designs reached a maximum complexity. There is more pecking than painting and typical designs are the flute player, mountain sheep, and elaborate blanket or pottery designs. The *kachina* figure and *kachina* mask appear at many sites, often identical with types still used in Southwest Indian ceremonies. Many recognizable birds are depicted both realistically and stylistically—the quail, duck, roadrunner, crane, and particularly the turkey and the eagle.

In August 1696, the Pueblo Indians of New Mexico, restless under the heavy hand of their conquerors, rose in rebellion, killed four hundred Spaniards, including twenty-one missionaries, and drove the remaining Spanish from the Pueblo country. The Spanish made repeated attempts to gain back their lost province and in 1692, Santa Fe and a number of pueblos capitulated. The aggressive Navajos from the northern plains, with a long record of preying on the Pueblo Indians, now made common cause with their old enemies against the Spanish; and much hard fighting followed. By 1695, peace was restored briefly, followed by a final rebellion the following year in the Rio Grande Valley. The revolt was unsuccessful and many Indians from the pueblos of San Cristobal, Pecos, Santa Clara, Jemez, San Ildefonso, and Cochiti fled to the Navajo country in the San Juan Valley.

In this refuge area, the two groups lived together peacefully and, as a result, the Navajos underwent an intensive acculturation. They adopted many Pueblo religious practices and paraphernalia, creation myths, matri-

Brown and white anthropomorph, Barrier Canyon, Utah. From photograph by Tom Mulhern.

lineal descent, manufacturing techniques (especially weaving), and even, for a time, the distinctive Pueblo architecture. The Navajo rock paintings and carvings that date from this time show many ideas borrowed from the Pueblos.

Examples of Navajo rock art are found in many of the sandstone canyons of the Four Corners region, especially in Gobernador, Carrizo, Largo, and Canon de Chelly. Many of their religious paintings are remarkably like the Pueblo *kachina* figures from seventeenth- and eighteenth-century kiva paintings.

The *kachinas* are supernatural beings or gods personified by dancers in ceremonies, many of which are connected with corn growing. The Navajo *yei* is the equivalent of the Pueblo *kachina*. There are examples of *yeis*, both painted and pecked, along several of the tributaries of the San Juan River in northern New Mexico. These figures are remarkably well drawn and are undoubtedly the forerunners of the superb figures later made by the Navajo in their sand paintings.

Some of the ceremonial figures in Navajo rock drawings can be identified by their similarity to those in modern sand paintings. The *yei* shown on page 121 is the hunchback god Ganaskidi, who carries a wand and the seeds of all vegetation in his feathered hump. Other recognizable eighteenth-century *yeis* are the Twin War Gods, often represented as shields, and a *yei* with peaked cap that resembles the Fringe Mouth Gods of the Night Chant myth.

There is evidence that many of the rock paintings and engravings marked Navajo sacred places or shrines where mythological events had occurred. According to Polly Schaafsma (1966), Navajos traveled to such a decorated spot at the confluence of the Pine and San Juan rivers as recently as the 1950s to hold ceremonies.

Aside from the Pueblo-style religious paintings, the Navajos continued to make their Plains-type hunting-magic drawings, featuring hunters, mounted horsemen, and realistic game animals (often with the heart-

Pecked "mastodon" near Moab, Utah. The last mastodons died out about 6,000 years ago.

Mummylike figures in shades of red-brown, Barrier Canyon, Utah. Photograph by Tom Mulhern.

Pueblo-type figures, San Juan River, northeastern New Mexico. Museum of New Mexico photograph.

Navajo drawing on a boulder (chalked) along the Piedra River, northwestern New Mexico. Museum of New Mexico photograph.

Corn plant and Navajo yei pecked on sandstone, Largo Canyon, northwestern New Mexico.

Navajo yei painting from the upper San Juan River area, New Mexico, 18th century. The colors are blue-gray, red, orange-yellow, rose, blue-green, and cream. Museum of New Mexico photograph.

line). The Navajo paintings in the Canyon de Chelly date from the 18th and 19th centuries and are quite naturalistic, showing Spaniards, horses, cattle, game animals, and the like. These are in association with typical Anasazi painted and pecked square-shouldered anthropomorphs, flute players, and hand prints.

These Navajo paintings and a few Apache paintings in eastern New Mexico are the only North American examples of the naturalistic poly-chrome style and closely resemble late historic Plains paintings on buffalo hides. The Navajo rock painters used a far broader range of colors than other North American tribes. In addition to the usual red, black, and white, they had blue-gray, blue-green, dark blue, yellow, orange, rose, and many shades of brown.

Pueblo-type pecked designs are plentiful in the Santa Fe-Albuquerque region of the Rio Grande, where basaltic rock takes the place of the dominant sandstone of the Four Corners region. In the Galisteo Basin south of Santa Fe, there is a major concentration of such designs and at one huge site covering a four-mile rock outcropping, there are hundreds of designs, including many masks and *kachina* figures. These cannot date later than about 1690, when the region was abandoned. At the eastern end of the basaltic dike, there are some very fine pecked shield drawings. They resemble 15th century kiva paintings at Pottery Mound near Albuquerque and may have been influenced by a migrating band from an area where such figures were traditional. In the Pueblo-type designs and also the shield panels, a dominant motif is the four-pointed star with a circular center. The star was traditionally drawn with four points by the American Indian—often by a simple cross or X. One of the many Hopi *kachinas* is Coto, the star-*kachina*, whose head is decorated with this symbol.

Abstract pecked design near El Paso, Texas. Redrawn from A. T. Jackson.

The eastern and southern New Mexico rock-art sites continue to reflect the general styles developed in the Four Corners region. A number of highly detailed and carefully painted sites, both naturalistic and stylized, have been attributed to Athabascan Apaches who were in possession of the country during the historic period.

Thanks to A. T. Jackson's excellent *Picture Writing of the Texas Indians*, we have a great deal of information on the large concentration of rock drawings in the region of southwest Texas bounded by the Rio Grande and Pecos rivers.

In the extreme western part of the state, there are painted sites with many designs reminiscent of the Pueblo country—masks, blanket and pottery designs, and mountain sheep. A famous site is at Hueco Tanks, a rocky area near El Paso. Here the paintings are around a number of large natural rock reservoirs. First described by Bartlett in 1854, it was a favorite stopping spot for the pioneer immigrant trains and later for

Shield motifs representing guardian spirits and clan symbols at Galisteo Basin, south of Santa Fe, New Mexico.

sightseers from El Paso. It has been badly vandalized but enjoys a measure of protection today as it is inside the Army lands at Fort Bliss.

Between the Hueco Tanks site and the Pecos River, there are a great many sites. The oldest are pecked designs similar to the typical Great Basin style with hand prints, meandering lines, and connected circles. The most recent-appearing drawings are realistic paintings, probably made by Apache Indians. An extensive site in this style is located on a large rock overhang by a spring, with many excellent paintings of mounted Indians, priests, thunderbirds, and animals, including a beautiful rendering of a deer.

Some of the most interesting paintings in the Southwest are found in the innumerable rock shelters near the junction of the Rio Grande and Pecos rivers. Over 75 per cent of the paintings are in a polychrome style. These intriguing pictures feature elongated figures usually without either faces or legs. Some of them resemble the mummylike creatures of eastern Utah. With them are stylized animals, especially antelope, cougar, insects, and plants. At some sites, historic paintings occur, undoubtedly made by the Apache. David Gebhard has described six styles from the Diablo area—the oldest, polychrome, followed by four differing red styles, and finally the historic realistic style. He suggests that the subject matter indicates not only hunting magic but also warfare magic as many of the human figures are pierced by spears and arrows.[1]

There are numerous pecked sites in central and southern Arizona featuring Pueblo design elements, with oustanding examples in the Petrified Forest National Park and south of Flagstaff along the Verde River. West of Phoenix, the drawings show strong Great Basin influence and the workmanship is much cruder—a large site near Gila Bend is in the curvilinear abstract style.

There are some immense gravel outline figures (see chapter 2) along the lower Colorado River in southeastern California. The best known are three very large spread-eagle human figures with two four-legged animals (coyotes?) and spirals in association with two of them. One writer has assumed the quadrupeds are horses and has dated them in historic times.[2] Personally I think that, with rare exceptions, the horse can be positively identified only if the artist has included the horseman. The largest human figure is 167 feet long and the creators could never have had an over-all look at their work as the only way it can be seen is from the air. The dark desert-varnish-covered stones are removed to bring out the figure detail in the light-colored sand beneath, and the removed stones are placed in ridges outlining the forms. These particular gravel drawings are in the territory of the Mojave but we do not know that these Indians were the artists. It is possibly significant that the gravel figures are located between the territories of the sand-painting people of the Southwest

Pecked design near Springville, Arizona. From photograph by Harold S. Gladwin.

Great Basin—type drawings, Newspaper Rock, Petrified Forest National Park, Arizona. Photograph by Richard O'Hanlon.

Fabric or pottery designs, Petrified Forest National Park, Arizona. Photograph by Richard O'Hanlon.

(Hopi, Navajo, Papago, Apache, etc.) and the sand-painting people of southern California (Luiseño, Diegueño, and Cahuilla).

The scope of the Southwest is so vast that it is difficult to do more than touch a few high spots. I have tried to orient the reader with geographical features rather than arbitrary political boundaries. In this next section, however, I will cover Mexico as a special unit of the Southwest.

With the exception of Baja California, we know almost nothing of the rock art of northern Mexico and until much more work is done, no firm conclusions can be drawn. It is only natural that the high cultures of Mexico with their dramatic ruins and superb artifacts have beguiled the archaeologists for over a hundred years to the almost complete exclusion of the lower culture areas to the north. A few articles have been written by French and Mexican investigators, but the map on page 17 is mostly blank for great sections of northern Mexico.

For most of our knowledge of the peninsula of Baja California, we are indebted to the investigations of Léon Diguet who in 1894 recorded many sites in central and southern Baja. In the northern mountain ranges, the few recorded sites are simple polychrome paintings done by the Diegueño Indians, whose territory extended several hundred miles south of the border. A number of pecked sites are known from the east side of the peninsula and these follow the Great Basin abstract tradition.

East of the forbidding, waterless Viscaíno Desert, there are a number of canyons cutting through the rugged mountains where sizable springs have created isolated palm oases. Diguet was the first to describe some extraordinary painted caves in these canyons. The dominant motif is the human figure, featureless and with raised arms. The figures are divided longitudinally or horizontally into red and black zones and are often life-sized or larger. Deer, mountain sheep, antelope, cougar, rabbits, and fish occur with the humans and are often very well drawn. At one site, there are many human figures pierced by arrows and figures drawn lying prone. These may represent warfare magic with all enemies happily full of arrows. In 1962, Erle Stanley Gardner, the author, prospecting the almost impassable country by helicopter, discovered a major site in this style. Since then a few more sites in the same tradition have been found by people stimulated by the publicity of Gardner's find. Clement Meighan, who made a survey of the site, has a radiocarbon date of over 500 years for a wooden artifact recovered in one of the caves. Other paintings in this section are chiefly abstract in red, black, and yellow.

The rock-pecked designs of southern Baja continue to resemble the Great Basin curvilinear abstract style, and in the mountains around La Paz there are a few simple paintings on isolated rocks. The subject matter includes hand prints, rabbits, and fish, a rare subject in rock art. All fish from Baja California are painted vertically, a convention that is found only here and across the Gulf of California in Sonora.

Red and white anthropomorphs, Sierra Santa Teressa, Sonora. These figures are about six inches high.

Several years ago, I heard of a painted site in coastal Sonora, roughly across the Gulf of California from the Baja caves with their large red-and-black figures. In the fall of 1965, I decided to investigate this site hoping to find a relationship to the Baja paintings. The Sonora paintings are in a most spectacular little gorge where the Sierra Santa Teressa rises from the coastal plain. For about a quarter of a mile, the stream, fed by the

Erle Stanley Gardner (second from left) examining large polychrome figures from a forty-four-foot panel, Sierra San Francisco, Baja California. Photograph courtesy of Erle Stanley Gardner.

summer rains, had cut a deep slit through the soft rhyolitic rock about 100 feet deep and 15 feet wide. On the almost sheer walls of the gorge and to a height of over 60 feet from the stream bed are innumerable paintings in red, white, black, and yellow. The styles were quite unlike anything in Baja California and much of the painting is in a style I have not seen anywhere else.

Many of the motifs in the bottom of the gorge, painted just above the summer flood-line, are of small anthropomorphic figures, none over a foot tall and slightly resembling the mummylike figures from eastern Utah. The bodies are long rectangles, with no arms and with three peg-like appendages in place of legs. The bodies are filled in with the most intricate and carefully executed geometric patterns, suggesting fabric designs. On the upper sections of the cliff there are many tiny human and animal drawings, some less than two inches long: horsemen, deer, dancing men with headdresses, hump-backed figures armed with bows, and hand prints. Everywhere there are beautiful geometric designs, usually enclosed in squares or rectangles. Suddenly in the center of many of the small paintings is a life-sized horseman with feathered headdress done in an entirely different style.

On the same trip we recorded eleven other sites in the region, including several on Tiburon Island and the adjacent coast. These latter are in the Seri territory and are very simple and crude compared to the Santa

Pecked drawing, Sierra de San Pablo, Sinaloa. Redrawn from A. Pompa y Pompa.

Deeply pecked designs near Saltillo, Coahuila. Photograph by Carl Compton.

Teressa sites—the paintings are of game animals and stylized humans in red and the pigment looks as though it was applied with the finger. Still another painting style, possibly also done by the Seris, is in black and white—animals and triangular human figures without legs. The fine geometric patterns may have been made by the Pima Baja, whose territory adjoins that of the Seri along the Sierra. (Woven headbands collected in Arizona in 1850 are quite similar.) Many of the paintings in this region are located at natural rock reservoirs (*tinajas*) that store the summer rains and provide the only water in this dry land.

Antonio Pompa y Pompa has recorded many painted sites in the State of Sinaloa. They are found in the Sierra from one end of the state to the other and the few published examples show them to be red and in the curvilinear abstract style. A few sites have been described from Durango. There are pecked and painted geometric designs inside squares and rectangles from Durango and simple abstract paintings in dots, circles, and diamond shapes near the Durango–Coahuila border.

The remaining examples known in northern Mexico are a few pecked sites in Coahuila with simple curvilinear abstract designs and some painted cave sites in the Sierra de Tamaulipas. The latter are rather carelessly executed drawings and are of two styles. The earliest are red and consist of short parallel lines, concentric circles, and hand prints. The second style dates from historic times (Tamaulipas was conquered by the Spanish in the late 18th century) and the crude drawings are in black of humans and horsemen. These are probably the work of hunting parties in the mountains and reflect nothing of the high culture of the Huaxtecs who lived in the fertile plains below the Sierra.[3]

All the rock-drawing styles listed in chapter 3 are found in the Southwest with the exception of the pit and groove and these may exist but have gone unrecorded. The central position of the Southwest made it the meeting ground of artistic traditions: abstract from the Great Basin to the west; naturalistic from the Columbia Plateau and the Plains to the north and east; and geometric abstract from Mexico to the south.

Pecked designs near Zape Chico, Durango. Redrawn from J. Alden Mason.

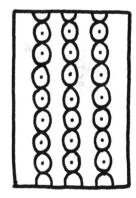

16 THE GREAT PLAINS

Incised warrior on horse, Milk River, Alberta. Redrawn from Selwyn Dewdney, 1964.

The vast area of the Great Plains, the heartland of the continent, is mainly prairie and grassland, bounded on the west by the Rocky Mountains and on the east by the forests of the Eastern Woodland. The great river of the plains is the Missouri, main tributary of the Mississippi with headwaters in the northern Rockies. The Northern Plains extend into southern Alberta, Saskatchewan, and Manitoba as far as the edge of the coniferous forests.

The typical Plains culture, dependent on buffalo hunting, dominated the entire area with the exception of south-central Texas. Before the introduction of the horse, the Northern Plains were sparsely inhabited and archaeological work in Nebraska and the Dakotas has shown an earlier culture of semisedentary people who made pottery and lived in square earth lodges. With the mobility made possible by the horse, tribes from the perimeter areas began to roam widely over the prairies following the buffalo. Prominent in this tremendous population shift were the Dakota (Sioux), Assiniboin, and Cheyenne from the northeastern Woodland; the Pawnee-Arikara and Wichita from the southeastern Woodland; and the Wind River Shoshone, Comanche, and Ute from the Great Basin. All these tribes gradually abandoned their earlier way of life and created the Plains culture. But even though these geographically diversified peoples created a common culture, their rock art often reflected the traditions of their origins.

A look at the map shows large sections of the Great Plains where no drawing sites have been recorded. This is mainly flat land with few suitable rock surfaces. There are, however, rock outcroppings, wind-eroded caves, and isolated boulders on which both paintings and carvings occur.

The rock drawings in Alberta with few exceptions lie along an old buffalo migration route taken by the immense herds moving up from Montana every year. Buffalo jumps are found along this route with rock pictures nearby. The painted sites are in the typical Algonquian style that was described in the Fraser-Columbia Plateau section. Red and black are the only colors and the drawings are crude naturalistic or stylized. The realistic subjects include humans, deer, buffalo, and bear; the stylized are shield figures, square-bodied anthropomorphs with V-neck, thunderbirds, and faces.

Glacial erratics have often been used by these Indians for their rock pictures. The rocks are sometimes painted but usually carved in the pit-and-groove style.

On the Milk River, a northern tributary of the Missouri, there is a major complex of sites. For several miles, spirited pictures are incised in the sandstone cliffs. These carvings follow the story-telling tradition of the Northern Plains so well-known from decorated buffalo robes. Successful hunts, combats between mounted and unmounted warriors, and battles are vividly portrayed. There are many examples of shield and V-necked figures, the latter often showing the heart-line. A few of the pictures are painted but most are deeply incised. This region was the territory of the Gros Ventre and the Blackfeet and these Indians probably made the rock drawings (though there is always the possibility in the plains that raiding parties from adjoining tribes made pictures outside their own country).

Red painting along buffalo migration route, near Cayley, southwestern Alberta. Redrawn from Douglas Leechman, Margaret Hess, and Roy L. Fowler.

Throughout the Northern Plains states of Montana, Wyoming, and the Dakotas, the shield figure, both painted and incised (in many cases, simply the shield), is the most prominent motif. The subject matter, aside from the shield symbols, is naturalistic, featuring game animals, hunters, and horsemen. It is certain that the majority of these Northern Plains drawings are of the historic period. Most of the Montana sites are very crudely painted with thick red lines suggesting finger application, and many of the scratched or incised drawings are mere scrawls. In North Dakota, there are animal forms made by pebble arrangements on the ground somewhat like the gravel pictures in southeastern California. These probably have an affinity with the effigy mounds of the Eastern Woodland.

In the Wind River country of central Wyoming, there is an entirely different situation. In an area centering on Riverton, there is a large concentration of rock-pecked designs totally unlike the realistic incised drawings of the Northern Plains. This is high desert and mountain country with many sandstone cliffs and outcroppings. The typical motif is a highly stylized anthropomorph with fantastic headdress and appendages. The outlined bodies are filled with abstract designs very reminiscent of the decorated anthropomorphs of southeastern California. This is the territory of the Wind River Shoshones whose origin in southeastern California and southern Nevada (see chapter 7) is further demonstrated

Pit-and-groove carvings, southern Alberta. From D. R. King and Selwyn Dewdney.

Pecked supernatural beings (chalked), northwestern Wyoming. Photograph by David Gebhard.

by their rock drawings. Abstract curvilinear drawings and the mountain-sheep motif so characteristic of the Great Basin occur along the Snake River, a natural migration route to the Wind River country.

To the east of the Bighorn River, the incised and painted Northern Plains styles are dominant, continuing through the Black Hills and the Missouri River basin of South Dakota, Sioux territory. In the eastern half of the state, there is an occasional pecked site in the Eastern Woodland style, with footprints, turkey tracks, and the like.

In southwestern Minnesota there are several interesting sites that appear

*Pecked anthropomorphs (chalked), Dinwoody Lakes, Wyoming. Photograph by David
Gebhard.*

to have been made by the Dakota prior to their Plains culture days. At
the Catlinite * quarries in Pipestone Country, there are many pecked and
abraded figures on the sandstone boulders. The forms are deeply cut and
include such motifs as men in bird costumes, buffalo, elk, and turtles. It
is possible that the figures are totems made by the Indians before quarry-
ing the catlinite.

Very few sites have been recorded in Nebraska, but in the northeast
corner of the state are several incised rocks that seem very much out of
place in the Great Plains. The drawings are of men dressed in bird costumes, hands, thunderbirds, bear tracks, turkey tracks, bisected circles,
and the Winnebago medicine animal (see chapter 4). How these Eastern
Woodland carvings happened to be in Nebraska is an interesting and

* Soft red stone much prized for pipe-making.

Naturalistic incised horses and riders (chalked), Hell Creek Valley, Kansas. Photograph by Thomas Witty.

depressing story. The Winnebago Indians, first described by the French in 1634 as living on Green Bay, Wisconsin, lost their ancient lands through a worthless treaty with the American government in 1825. In the following years, they were repeatedly moved from reservation to reservation as the land-hungry whites pushed farther west. In 1863, their final move brought them to a reservation in northeast Nebraska. The rock drawings therefore cannot be earlier than that date.

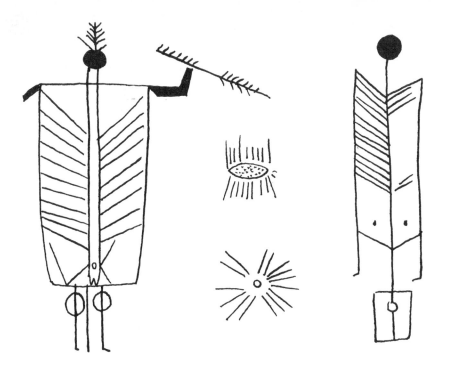

*Stylized incised figures,
Rice County, Kansas.
Redrawn from Wedel.*

The rock drawings of the central Great Plains reflect traditions from all the surrounding areas. In eastern Colorado, the Oklahoma Panhandle, and northeastern New Mexico, there is a strong Great Basin influence. The Shoshonean Utes occupied much of this territory and their origin shows in their rock-drawing style. In Kansas, central Oklahoma, and western Missouri, there is a transition zone between the naturalistic style of the Plains with its horsemen, shield figures, and game animals, and the earlier Woodland style featuring thunderbirds, footprints, and game tracks.

In Texas, the Panhandle and the central part of the state were Comanche territory, marking the farthest penetration east of the aggressive Shoshoneans in prehistoric times. There is no evidence of the Great Basin style here and the Comanche must have brought no rock-drawing tradition with them. The rock-incised pictures from the Panhandle are quite realistic, showing a strong Northern Plains influence, but farther south all but a few sites are painted in styles that seem to have originated in the Pecos-Rio Grande region. Many designs are elaborate abstractions and some are in polychrome. Historic period drawings of mission buildings, mounted men, and cattle are common and they are done in a realistic style with the figures solidly filled in with color, usually red.

Most of the rock drawings that are clearly in the typical Plains incised style occur in the Northern Plains. The situation in the Central and Southern Plains is very complex, reflecting strong influences from the Eastern Woodland and from the Southwest (particularly the Big Bend country of the Rio Grande).

*Pecked footprints and
abstract designs near
Tulare, South Dakota.*

17 THE EASTERN WOODLAND

Pecked bird with speech symbol, eastern Missouri. From photograph by Frank Magre.

This region includes most of the hardwood forests in the United States, and with its ample water and game, was a hunter's paradise supporting large hunting and food-gathering populations. The map on page 17 shows relatively few rock-drawing sites compared to the western section of the country. Parts of 31 states are included in the region, nine of which have no drawings at all. Most of the sites are concentrated along the Mississippi and some large tributaries, the Ohio, Kanawha, and Tennessee rivers.

To understand the rock-art situation in the Eastern Woodland it will be well to review briefly the history of the Woodland Indians. By 2500 B.C. Algonquian-speaking people moving into the New World had reached the Eastern Woodland, bringing with them two basic cultural traits (also found in Siberia): burial mounds and cord-marked pottery. These hunters and food gatherers occupied the river valleys, especially the upper Mississippi and Ohio drainages.

About 500 B.C. a spectacular culture was developing in the Illinois and Ohio valleys—a culture known to archaeologists as Hopewell after an enormous burial mound in Ohio. These people practiced agriculture and had an advanced technology, including large ceremonial flints, elaborately carved stone pipes, and ornaments in copper and silver. This culture had a wide influence on areas as far west as eastern Iowa and Missouri.

In the Southeast around A.D. 900 a new culture was developing from the earlier Woodland tradition. This was the Mississippi culture patterned after the Mexican civilizations in Middle America. Whether these influences spread through trade or Mexican settlements along the Gulf of Mexico, we do not know, but such startling innovations as huge pyramid temple mounds, highly organized towns, and systematic corn agriculture radically altered the pattern of life. The nearest high Mexican culture is that of the Huaxtecs in Tamaulipas State. Engraved shell gorgets from there are strikingly similar to some found in Missouri and Tennessee. By the time De Soto made his brutal march through the area in 1540, many large ceremonial centers had been built and the people were living in palisaded towns. The largest of these centers was Cahokia in southern Illinois, with others at Spiro, Oklahoma; Moundville, Alabama; and Etowah, Georgia. These people were of the Hokan-language stock, occupying at this time all of southeastern United States, and the principal tribes were the Cherokee, Creek, Choctaw, and Chickasaw. By 1400 a dynamic segment of the southeastern Hokan had migrated to the Northeast and had driven a wedge through the Algonquian tribes to the Saint Lawrence River. These were the Iroquois and they took with them their well-organized political system, fortified towns, and agricultural practices.

Most of the rock pictures in the Eastern Woodland are near the ceremonial centers of the Hopewell and Mississippi cultures but with few exceptions they bear little resemblance to the art forms of these cultures. The petroglyphs are almost invariably deeply incised or pecked, sometimes to a depth of over an inch. The technique and subject matter are very similar over the entire Eastern Woodland with some local variations, and the most abundant motifs are the thunderbird, hands, footprints, animal and turkey tracks.

In the upper Mississippi drainage where Minnesota, Wisconsin, and Iowa meet, there are many sites featuring these designs with deer, beaver, fish, and men as additional elements. According to an old Ojibwa who was interviewed in the 1880's, these represented totem marks. In this same region, there are many large effigy mounds in the shape of humans, animals, birds, and snakes, monuments to an obsessive cult for honoring the dead.

The only large concentration of rock drawings in the Eastern Woodland is in Missouri, near the junction of the Missouri and Mississippi rivers. Innumerable deeply pecked designs are found on the horizontal surfaces of limestone bedrock, usually in hilly and forested land. The thunderbird is the dominant design element but hand- and foot-prints, humans, arrows, and bird tracks are abundant. The thunderbird must have played a major part in the ceremonies of these Indians. Many of the drawings suggest a man in bird costume and shamans may have personated the deity during certain rituals.

The Cahokia Mound, largest earth pyramid north of Mexico (100 feet high and covering 16 acres), is located in Illinois just across the river from

Pecked footprints, Belmont County, Ohio. Redrawn from Garrick Mallery, 1893.

Pecked figures, Winona County, Minnesota. Redrawn from Dean R. Snow.

Pecked designs on limestone boulder, northeastern Missouri. Photograph by Frank Magre.

Red painting of bilobed arrow, Washington County, Missouri. From photograph by Frank Magre.

Pecked fertility symbols, Washington State Park, Missouri. From photograph by Frank Magre.

Deeply pecked figures on limestone bedrock, northeastern Missouri. Photograph by Frank Magre.

Pecked drawings of fish and deer, Salt River, northeastern Missouri. Photograph by Allen Eichenberger.

Meandering patterns (chalked) incised and pecked on steatite, known as the Judaculla Rock, near Sylva, North Carolina. Photograph by Ewart Ball.

many of the Missouri sites, and motifs connected with this Mississippi ceremonial center are depicted in a few of the rock drawings such as the baton (exactly like the ceremonial flint batons excavated in many sites), and the bilobed arrow, a well-known cult symbol of the Mississippi culture. Carvings of these two symbols are also found in Tennessee and Alabama.

Other motifs in the same area that suggest Mississippi culture influence are birds with speech symbols coming from their beaks, bisected horseshoe shapes that may be fertility symbols (see page 138), and various forms of spindles that suggest the plummets or charmstones found in many parts of the Mississippi Valley and in California. A circular arrangement of one of these designs is reminiscent of similar circular arrangements of charmstones described from ceremonies of the Chumash and Yokuts in California.

There is a change of style in the Tennessee Valley, northern Georgia, and adjoining North Carolina. It is basically an elaboration on the pit-and-groove style of the western states, with added concentric circles, meandering lines, and occasional animal tracks. The most elaborate is the Judaculla Rock, North Carolina, a large carved steatite boulder. These pit-and-groove sites may be the oldest examples of rock drawing in the Eastern Woodland. Some Georgia sites show extensive erosion on designs pecked into hard granite. An interesting incised stone was found in Tennessee. It is not at all typical of the rock drawings of the region, rather resembling the Mississippi culture engravings on shell, and shows costumes, weapons, and utensils.

In the Kanawha Valley of West Virginia there were many sites described by Mallery in 1893, but they have been destroyed through dam building and road construction. A number of sites in the upper Ohio Valley near Wheeling feature meandering lines, round-headed anthropomorphs, turkey and animal tracks, and footprints. Other examples occur in Rhode Island and at the celebrated Dighton Rock in Massachusetts. This site, identical in style and technique to examples in Pennsylvania, has been discussed by armchair antiquarians for centuries (even Cotton Mather made a rather bad drawing of it in 1712), and all sorts of explanations have been offered. It has been ascribed to the Scythians, Phoenicians, and the Norsemen. Lately a new theory has appeared: the rock, moved from its original site (see chapter 9), has been placed in a small park with an adjoining display proving that the round-headed anthropomorphs are actually part of the Portuguese coat of arms, and the whole inscription is a message from Miguel Cortereal, a Portuguese explorer. The Algonquian Indians who incised the lines at least 350 years ago would have been amused.

Vast areas around Lake Michigan were occupied by Algonquian tribes

Incised stone tablet nineteen by fifteen inches found on Rocky Creek near Nashville, Tennessee. Retouched in white ink. Redrawn from Garrick Mallery, 1893.

such as the Miami and the Potawatomi. There are only a few isolated sites known in this country, which is curious as surrounding tribes made many rock pictures. In Michigan, there are two—a cliff painting in the northern part of the state done in the Northern Woodland style, and an extensive pecked and incised site in eastern Michigan. The figures are cut into sandstone bedrock and include all the main Eastern Woodland motifs with the addition of the medicine animal or water panther.

Many examples of the typical Algonquian thunderbird occur at sites in the Mississippi Valley from southern Minnesota to the junction of the Mississippi with the Ohio. The only other occurrence of this distinctive symbol in the Eastern Woodland is at Safe Harbor in Pennsylvania. The

Pecked animals, tracks, and anthropomorphs, Millsboro, Pennsylvania. Site now destroyed. Redrawn from Garrick Mallery, 1893.

Pecked designs on Dighton Rock, near Dighton, Massachusetts, from drawing made in 1830. Redrawn from Garrick Mallery, 1893.

rock design elements that can be positively linked with the Mississippi culture are the birds with speech symbols, batons, and bilobed arrows that occur at Missouri and Alabama sites. Only in eastern Missouri near the Cahokia Mound do the thunderbird and the Mississippi symbols occur together. Apparently the southeastern Indians did not share the thunderbird cult symbol with their Algonquian neighbors.

There are problems connected with dating in the Eastern Woodland. A great many of the sites are carved on horizontal surfaces of exposed bedrock, often limestone. When the drawings were freshly cut, there was undoubtedly contrast between the patinated rock and the design areas. In the humid eastern climate, however, patination and lichen growth occur rapidly, destroying all contrast and making these carvings almost impossible to photograph without chalking. This rapid patination makes relative dating difficult, as everything has the same tone. There is only one site showing evidence of European contact, suggesting that the practice of rock drawing died out slightly after the white invasions.

As a rule the Eastern Woodland rock drawings lack careful workmanship or design but there are exceptions, like the running men on page 138 and some of the concentric circle patterns from Georgia (neither of which are typical of the Eastern Woodland).

Many of the Missouri designs were probably cult symbols that had magical as well as religious meaning, and participation in rituals at a decorated rock might have imparted the power of the symbol to the participants. There are few drawings of game animals, but in some areas animal and bird tracks might have been connected with hunting magic.

Pecked Algonquin thunderbird and other figures, Safe Harbor, Susquehanna River, Pennsylvania. Site is now destroyed. Redrawn from D. Cadzow.

Red and yellow painting, Jackson County, Alabama. Redrawn from J. W. Cambron and S. A. Waters.

EASTERN WOODLAND STYLES (PECKED AND INCISED)

Style	Locations	Main design elements
Woodland Naturalistic	Mississippi Valley north of Ohio Valley	Thunderbird, hand- and foot-prints, animal and turkey tracks
Woodland Stylized	Ohio Valley Rhode Island	Round-headed anthropomorphs, animals, footprints, tracks, snakes, meandering lines
Woodland Pit and Groove	Tennessee Valley and adjoining areas	Dots, concentric circles, tracks, meandering lines
Mississippi Stylized	Eastern Missouri Tennessee Valley	Batons, bilobed arrows, various abstract forms

There are a few scattered painted sites, mainly naturalistic, from the northern or Algonquian region, and a number of abstract painted sites from Hokan territory in the Tennessee Valley.

18 THE NORTHERN WOODLAND

Nearly all of the rock drawings of the Northern Woodland appear on the Canadian Shield, a roughly shield-shaped mass of Precambrian rocks that covers nearly half of Canada and large areas in the northern United States (see map on page 146). There are innumerable lakes and rivers on the Shield, and there is perhaps more water than land in most areas. These conditions made water travel imperative and the famous birch-bark canoe was used by all the Northern Woodland tribes. It is a heavily forested land, mostly coniferous but with deciduous trees in the southern transition zone.

The major part of the Shield region was occupied by the Algonquian-speaking tribes, and the most important of these were the Ojibwa and the Cree. The southeastern edge of the Shield was in the territory of the Hurons, part of the Iroquoian migration from the Mississippi region, and the northwestern Shield was part of the Athabascan country (the area from which the Athabascan Navajo and Apache had migrated).

The Indians of the Northern Woodland were hunters of deer, elk, caribou, moose, and occasionally buffalo. Lacking pottery, they made use of the canoe birch for containers of all kinds. This same indispensable tree furnished material for bark scrolls used in mnemonic records, and for the toboggans dragged by men on snowshoes. They traveled in small bands and their ceremonial life, dictated by the group leader or shaman, must have been of the simplest nature.

The Algonquian tribes occupied a wide territory from the Pacific Northwest to Newfoundland and their hunting and food-gathering cul-

Red painting of caribou, Rattler Creek, Saskatchewan. From photograph by Tim Jones.

145

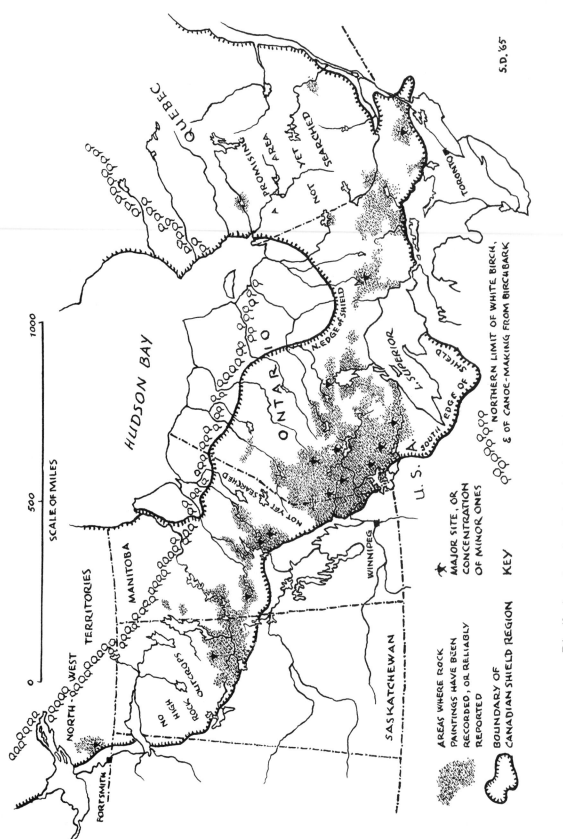

Distribution of rock paintings in the Canadian Shield area of the Northern Woodland. Map by Selwyn Dewdney.

The following labels appear on the map:

S.D. '65

QUEBEC

HUDSON BAY

ONTARIO

MANITOBA

NORTH · WEST TERRITORIES

SASKATCHEWAN

WINNIPEG

TORONTO

FORT SMITH

L. SUPERIOR

U.S.A.

NO HIGH ROCK OUTCROPS

N. EDGE of SHIELD

SOUTH EDGE OF SHIELD

A PROMISING AREA NOT YET SEARCHED

NOT YET SEARCHED

NORTHERN LIMIT OF WHITE BIRCH, & of CANOE-MAKING FROM BIRCH BARK

SCALE OF MILES

0   500   1000

KEY

MAJOR SITE, OR CONCENTRATION OF MINOR ONES

AREAS WHERE ROCK PAINTINGS HAVE BEEN RECORDED, OR RELIABLY REPORTED

BOUNDARY OF CANADIAN SHIELD REGION

ture was remarkably the same wherever they went. Their rock drawings both in style and technique are in the same tradition from coast to coast and are like those of the Salish described in the Columbia-Fraser Plateau section. The style is predominantly naturalistic though there are many unidentified motifs. In most cases they seem to have applied the red pigment with their fingers.

Almost everything we know of these drawings has come from the excellent surveys by Selwyn Dewdney, who has been recording sites on the Shield since 1957. His field work has been by canoe and plane and considering the immense territory to be covered, he has obviously only scratched the surface. He reports that a great many paintings must have been done from canoes.

Large concentrations of paintings have been described from Ontario Province, particularly in the Lake-of-the-Woods region, and on both sides of the Ontario-Minnesota border. Aside from many unrecognizable objects, the most abundant motifs in that area are manned canoes, thunderbirds, hands, buffalo, bear, elk, moose, humans (often in ceremonial or shaman's costume), and supernatural beings. Historical subjects are rare and date from the French and English occupations. These include men with rifles, European forts, boats, and horsemen. At a few sites there are human figures smoking pipes.

Many Woodland tribes belived in an all-powerful deity, the Great Spirit or Manitou. This major supernatural figure was never personified in drawings but lesser deities figure on the rocks. The Ojibwa have a mischievous being called Maymaygwayshi, who lives in cracks and shallow caves along the water. He is very fond of fish and often robs the traps of the Indians. This spirit appears as a short, large-headed creature, sometimes with horns. The Ojibwa shaman was supposed to have the power to enter rocks and trade tobacco with the spirit for "rock medicine." [1] Other deities were the Thunderer (thunderbird); Missikinahpik, the Great Serpent; and Mishipizhiw, the Great Water Lynx. The latter is known by many names such as water panther and water monster and is the same creature as the medicine animal of the Winnebago. This sinister being was all-powerful in swift or rough water and his aid might be solicited if a dangerous water crossing was in prospect (see chapter 4). The Indians still leave small offerings such as clothing, tobacco, and bundles of colored sticks at painted rock sites. The sites are regarded as spirit rocks and the gifts are to placate the supernatural beings or to obtain their good will. Local Ojibwa have said that the offerings were made when someone was sick, different colors symbolizing different ailments. Other informants said that the offerings were for "good luck." This sort of thing is widespread in aboriginal America. In the Chumash region of southern California, the Indians often built little shrines of

Red painting of buffalo transmitting power to man, Churchill River, Saskatchewan. Redrawn from Selwyn Dewdney, 1963.

sticks and brush in which they would leave cloth, tobacco, and other articles as presents for the unseen spirits.

The drawings were doubtless made for a variety of reasons. The Salish in the Columbia-Fraser Plateau made drawings as records of dreams (see chapter 4), and this custom may have been followed in the Northern Woodland. The drawing on page 147 shows a man getting "power" from a buffalo; the power was thought to be transmitted through dreams or visions. Occasionally the pictures told a story, as in the painting of the raid across Lake Superior described in chapter 4. The large numbers of game-animal drawings suggest the hunting-magic motivation so common in the western United States. Some motifs may be clan symbols.

There are a few rock-pecked sites that have been described from Ontario and northern Minnesota. These are usually on horizontal surfaces and are crudely pecked animals, thunderbirds, and humans similar to the examples in southern Minnesota.

Investigations in the Shield country of northern Manitoba and Saskatchewan are now under way and over 50 sites have been recorded. Many of these are on the Churchill River drainage with its outlet on Hudson Bay, a region whose infinite number of lakes connected by streams or short portages make it a canoer's paradise. The paintings are in the same style as those in Ontario. There is one site with a striking drawing of a bear-headed shaman. One painting shows a man shooting a moose with a gun. The thunderbird continues as a major motif. This is mainly Cree country, a tribe with close ties with the Ojibwa, though the Churchill River region is also shared by Athabascan people. Several sites were recorded by Dewdney in 1965 between Fort Smith and Great Slave Lake in the Northwest Territories. These northernmost Shield sites seem to be in the same tradition as the Saskatchewan paintings and are in the territory of the Athabascan Slave Indians.

The only rock paintings from central Alaska are located on the Tanana River near Fairbanks. They depict human figures; several are inside a circle and others are in a boat that looks like a prowed dugout. This type of boat was used in southeastern Alaska.

There are a few carved sites in the Northern Woodland and the most interesting are in Nova Scotia, in the vicinity of Lake Kedgemakooge, where many rock drawings were made by the Micmac Indians. These are scratched on slabs of a smooth, slaty rock and the subjects include hands and feet, birds, animals, shields, headdresses, wigwams, etc.

A great many more paintings remain to be found in the Northern Woodland (Quebec Province, for example, has not been searched at all), but the vastness of the country, the difficulty of transportation, and the climate are formidable barriers to all but experienced and well-organized survey teams.

Scratched design by Mimac Indians, Kedgemakooge Lake, Nova Scotia. Redrawn from Garrick Mallery, 1893.

Female figure, possibly shaman, northern Saskatchewan. Photograph by Selwyn Dewdney.

STYLE CLASSIFICATION BY AREAS

	Far North	Northwest	Columbia-Fraser Plat.	Great Basin	California	Southwest	Great Plains	Eastern Woodland	Northern Woodland
PAINTED									
Naturalistic	X	X	X	X	X	X	X	X	X
Naturalistic Polychrome						X	X		
Stylized		X	X	X	X	X	X		X
Stylized Polychrome					X	X	X		
Abstract Linear			X	X	X	X			X
Abstract Polychrome			X	X	X	X			
PECKED									
Naturalistic			X	X		X	X	X	X
Stylized	X	X	X	X		X	X	X	X
Abstract Curvilinear			X	X	X	X		X	
Abstract Rectilinear			X	X		X	X		
Pit and Groove				X	X		X	X	
INCISED OR SCRATCHED									
Realistic *				X		X	X		X

* There are a few scattered examples of incised stylized and abstract but not enough to be classed as a main catogory.

CONCLUSIONS

In order to compress so complex a subject into a single volume it was necessary to cut the material to the bone. Many areas that would take several books to describe thoroughly have been allotted a paragraph or two.

One advantage, however, of so broad a study is that it is possible to show the extraordinary diversity of styles, techniques, and subjects created by the prehistoric North American Indians and how the different cultures each developed their characteristic rock-art forms.

Some styles were homogeneous over vast areas, such as the realistic painted tradition in the Algonquian territory stretching from Vancouver Island to Nova Scotia. Others, like the parti-colored figures in central Baja California, are confined to a few desert canyons.

Certain styles have been carried long distances by migrating tribes. The best examples of this are the Great Basin styles introduced into many areas by nomadic Shoshoneans. As contact was made with neighboring tribes having a rock-drawing tradition, there was a borrowing of ideas affecting style and subject matter but rarely technique. The Shoshoneans who pecked their designs on Great Basin basaltic rock continued their pecking technique on the sandstone of the Southwest.

There is no doubt that most of the rock drawings figured in ceremonies connected with the relation of man to the world around him, particularly the supernatural world. Specifically many of the pictures were made as visualizations of dreams during puberty rites or as hunting magic undertaken prior to a hunt.

Hunting magic was apparently not employed unless the quarry was a difficult animal to bag and a little supernatural aid was called for. There are innumerable pecked and incised drawings of the mountain sheep, a fine food animal and one of the wariest of beasts. If the game was plentiful, it rarely occurred in rock drawings. In southern Alberta, where enormous herds of buffalo migrated every year, drawings of the animal are almost nonexistent. Along the Columbia River where the Indians depended on the salmon as their main food supply, the easily procured fish was seldom pictured.

The most widespread design motif in North America, and indeed almost anywhere in the world where rock pictures are found, is the hand. It is a basic identifying sign for man, unmistakable and striking, from the Paleolithic caveprints made 30,000 years ago to the identical prints made in the Arizona canyons by the Navajo in historic times.

As the section on dating indicated, it is extremely difficult to tell the age of rock drawings though relative chronologies can be determined. The earliest rock-art sites in North America appear to be in the Great Basin, particularly southeastern California. The oldest style in the country is probably the pit and groove. This style is widely dispersed and the patterns are almost invariably pecked on isolated boulders.

The question of which Indians made which drawings can never have an entirely satisfactory answer. The constantly shifting populations in prehistoric America, with accompanying exchanges of cultural traits and art traditions, make the problem difficult indeed. However certain broad conclusions can be made. Through such clues as linguistic studies, association of drawings with archaeological remains, subject matter, and ethnographic information, we know what sort of culture produced each rock-art style and in many cases of the late prehistoric and historic periods, we know exactly what tribes made the pictures. We have convincing evidence of authorship for the Chumash and Luiseño in California, the Thompson River Salish in British Columbia, and the Hopi and Navajo in the Southwest, to name a few.

I have presented all the evidence available on the interpretation of these prehistoric drawings and in a general way we know why they were made. Only the original artist or shaman, however, would know the precise meanings of the pictures, and it is doubtful if many of us would understand him if he were here to explain. The world of the aboriginal Indian, where the supernatural was as real as the natural, is a world we cannot enter but nothing prevents us from enjoying the intriguing pictures that still exist by the thousands in caves and on cliffs.

NOTES*

CHAPTER I

1. Kenneth Macgowan, *Early Man in the New World*, p. 196.
2. Richard S. MacNeish, "The Origins of New World Civilization," pp. 29–37.
3. M. McKusick, *Men of Ancient Iowa*, p. 81.
4. Macgowan, *op. cit.*, p. 241.

CHAPTER 2

1. Douglas Leechman *et al.*, *Some Pictographs of Southeastern British Columbia*, p. 77.

CHAPTER 3

1. Christy G. Turner, *Petrographs of the Glen Canyon Region*, p. 1.
2. David Gebhard, "Petroglyphs of Wyoming: A Preliminary Paper."
3. Frederica de Laguna, *Chugach Prehistory*.

CHAPTER 4

1. D. S. Davidson, *Aboriginal Australian and Tasmanian Rock Carvings and Paintings*, pp. 124, 125.
2. James A. Teit, *A Rock Painting of the Thompson River Indians, British Columbia*.
3. Robert F. Heizer, *Sacred Rain Rocks of Northern California*, pp. 33–38.
4. Edward L. Keithahn, "The Petroglyphs of Southeastern Alaska."
5. De Laguna, *op. cit.*, p. 105.
6. Selwyn Dewdney and Kenneth E. Kidd, *Indian Rock Paintings of the Great Lakes*, p. 14.
7. H. S. Colton, *Black Sand—Prehistory in Northern Arizona*, pp. 80, 81.

CHAPTER 6

1. G. B. M. Flamand, *Les Pierres écrites . . .*
2. C. B. Hunt, *Desert Varnish*.

* Complete publishing information can be found in Bibliography.

3. B. P. Dutton, *Sun Father's Way—The Kiva Murals of Kuaua*, pp. 19–34.

4. Ronald E. Beschel, "Dating Rock Surfaces by Lichen Growth and Its Application to Glaciology and Physiography," pp. 1044–1062.

5. Gerhard Folmann, "Lichenometrische Altersbestimmungen an Vorchristlichen Steinsetzungen der Polynesischen Osterinsel."

6. Robert F. Heizer and Martin A. Baumhoff, *Prehistoric Rock Art of Nevada and Eastern California*, pp. 231, 232.

7. Turner, *op. cit.*, pp. 1–74.

CHAPTER 7

1. W. J. Sollas, *Ancient Hunters*, pp. 238–243.

2. J. V. Young, *The Peregrinations of Kokopelli*, pp. 39–41.

3. Colton, "Is the House of Tcuhu the Minoan Labyrinth?"

CHAPTER 11

1. R. M. Underhill, *Red Man's America*, p. 294.

2. G. T. Emmons, *Petroglyphs in Southeastern Alaska*, pp. 223, 224.

CHAPTER 13

1. Zenas Leonard, *Narrative of the Adventures of Zenas Leonard*, pp. 72, 73.

2. Heizer and Baumhoff, *op. cit.*, pp. 202–208.

CHAPTER 15

1. Gebhard, *Prehistoric Paintings of the Diablo Region of Western Texas*, p. 53.

2. F. M. Setzler, "Seeking the Secret of the Giants."

3. MacNeish, "Preliminary Investigations in the Sierra de Tamaulipas, Mexico," pp. 134–136.

CHAPTER 18

1. Dewdney and Kidd, *op. cit.*, p. 14.

SUGGESTED READING*

CAIN, H. THOMAS. *Petroglyphs of Central Washington.*

CRESSMAN, L. S. *Petroglyphs of Oregon.*

DEWDNEY, SELWYN, and KIDD, KENNETH E. *Indian Rock Paintings of the Great Lakes.*

GEBHARD, DAVID. *Prehistoric Paintings of the Diablo Region of Western Texas.*

GRANT, CAMPBELL. *The Rock Paintings of the Chumash.*

HEIZER, ROBERT F., and BAUMHOFF, MARTIN A. *Prehistoric Rock Art of Nevada and Eastern California.*

JACKSON, A. T. *Picture-Writing of Texas Indians.*

MALLERY, GARRICK. *Picture Writing of the American Indians.*

SCHAAFSMA, POLLY. *Rock Art of the Navajo Reservoir District.*

STEWARD, JULIAN H. *Petroglyphs of California and Adjoining States.*

————. *Petroglyphs of the United States.*

TURNER, CHRISTY G. *Petrographs of the Glen Canyon Region.*

---

* Complete publishing information can be found in Bibliography.

BIBLIOGRAPHY

Pecked mythical fish,
Sproat Lake, Vancouver
Island. Redrawn from
Garrick Mallery, 1893.

ANATI, E. *Camonica Valley*. New York: Alfred A. Knopf, 1961.

ANGEL, MYRON. *La Piedra Pintada*. Los Angeles: Grafton Publishing Co., 1910.

ARTHUR, GEORGE. *Pictographs in Central Montana*. Part III: *Comments*. Montana State University, Anthropology and Sociology Papers, No. 21. Missoula, 1960.

BANDI, H. G. *et al. The Art of the Stone Age*. New York: Crown Publishers, 1961.

BEATY, J. J. "The Petroglyph Puzzle," *Pacific Discovery*, Vol. XVI, No. 3 (May–June 1963).

BECKWITH, F. "Group of Petroglyphs Near Moab, Utah," *El Palacio* (Santa Fe), XXXVI, Nos. 23–24 (1934), 177–8.

———. "Ancient Indian Petroglyphs of Utah," *ibid.*, XXXVIII, Nos. 6–9 (1935), 33–40.

———. "Glyphs That Tell the Story of an Ancient Migration," *Desert Magazine* (El Centro), III, No. 10 (1940), 4–7.

BESCHEL, RONALD E. "Dating Rock Surfaces by Lichen Growth and Its Application to Glaciology and Physiography (Lichenometry)," in G. O. Raasch, ed., *Geology of the Arctic*, Vol. II. Toronto: University of Toronto Press, 1961.

BOLTON, H. E., and MARSHALL, T. M. *The Colonization of North America 1492–1783*. New York: The Macmillan Company, 1922.

BREUIL, H. *Four Hundred Centuries of Cave Art*. Montignac, Dordogne: Centre d'Études et de Documentation Préhistoriques, 1952.

BREWER, J., and BREWER, S. "Wupatki Petroglyphs," U.S. National Park Service Southwestern Monuments Monthly Report (Santa Fe), August 1935, pp. 129–32.

BROWNLEE, RICHARD S. "The Big Moniteau Bluff Pictographs in Boone County, Missouri," *The Missouri Archaeologist*, Vol. XVIII, No. 4 (December 1956).

BRUFF, J. G. "Indian Engravings on Rocks Along Green River Valley in Sierra Nevada Range of Mountains," *Annual Report of the Smithsonian Institution*. Washington, D.C., 1872, pp. 409–12.

BURKITT, M. C. *South Africa's Past in Stone and Paint*. Cambridge: Cambridge University Press, 1928.

CADZOW, D. *Petroglyphs in the Susquehanna River near Safe Harbor, Pennsylvania*. Publication of the Pennsylvania Historical Commission, Vol. III (1934).

CAIN, H. THOMAS. *Petroglyphs of Central Washington*. Seattle: University of Washington Press, 1950.

CALDWELL, WARREN W. "An Archeological Survey of the Okanagan and Similkameen Valleys of British Columbia," *Anthropology in British Columbia* (Provincial Museum, Victoria) No. 4, 1953–54.

CAMBRON, J. W., and WATERS, S. A. "Petroglyphs and Pictographs in the Tennessee Valley and Surrounding Area," *Journal of Alabama Archaeology*, Vol. V, Issue 2 (1959).

CARSTENS, C. J., and KNUDSEN, J. P. "Petroglyphs and Pictographs of the Tennessee Valley, Part II, Spectrographic Analysis of Pigments," *ibid*.

CHAPMAN, C., and CHAPMAN, E. F. *Indians and Archaeology of Missouri*. Columbia: University of Missouri Press, 1964.

CHAPMAN, C. E. *A History of California: The Spanish Period*. New York: The Macmillan Company, 1921.

CHAPMAN, K. M. "Pajaritan pictography: The Cave Pictographs of the Rito de los Frijoles," in Hewett, *Pajarito Plateau and Its Ancient People*. Handbooks of Archaeological History. Albuquerque, 1938. Appendix 1, pp. 139–148.

COLTON, H. S. *Black Sand—Prehistory in Northern Arizona*, Albuquerque: University of New Mexico Press, 1960.

———. "Is the House of Tcuhu the Minoan Labyrinth?" *Science* (Washington, D.C.), n.s. XLV, No. 1174 (1917), 667–668.

COLTON, M. R. F., and COLTON, H. S. "Petroglyphs, the Record of a Great Adventure," *American Anthropologist*, XXX, No. 1 (1931), 32–37.

CONNER, STUART W. *A Preliminary Survey of Prehistoric Picture Writing on Rock Surfaces in Central and South Central Montana*. Billings Archaeological Society, Anthropological Paper, No. 2, 1962.

———. "The Fish Creek, Owl Canyon, and Grinnvoll Rock Shelter Pictograph Sites in Montana," *Plains Anthropologist* (Journal of the Plains Conference) (Billings Archaeological Society Paper, 1962).

COSGROVE, C. B. *Caves of the Upper Gila and Hueco Areas in New Mexico and Texas*. Papers of the Peabody Museum, Vol. XXIV, No. 2. Cambridge: Harvard University Press, 1947.

COXON, W. "Ancient Manuscripts on American Stones," *Arizona Highways*, September 1964.

CRAWFORD, L. F. *History of North Dakota*, Vol. I. Chicago and New York: American Historical Society, 1931, pp. 36–37.

CRESSMAN, L. S. *Petroglyphs of Oregon*. University of Oregon Publications in Anthropology. Eugene, 1937.

CUTLER, H. E. "Medicine Men and the Preservation of a Relic Gene in Maize," *Journal of Heredity*, XXXV (1944), 290–94.

DAHLGREN, B., and ROMERO, J. "La Prehistoria Baja California Redescubrimiento de Pinturas Rupestres," *Cuadernos Americanos*, LVIII (1951), 153–178.

DAHLGREN DE JORDAN, B. "Las Pinturas Rupestres de la Baja California," *Artes de Mexico*, No. 3, March, April 1954.

DANCKER, DOROTHY. "Black Hills Vacationers Puzzled by Centuries-Old Indian Carvings; Origin of Artists Remains Mystery," *The Daily Plainsman* (Huron, South Dakota), August 2, 1964.

D'ANGLURE, SALADIN. "Decouverte de petroglyphes a Qajartalik sur Ille de Qikertaaluk," (Ottawa, Department of Northern Affairs and National Resources), IX, No. 6 (1962), 34–39.

DAVIDSON, D. S. *Aboriginal Australian and Tasmanian Rock Carvings and Paintings.* Memoirs of the American Philosophical Society, Vol. V, Philadelphia, 1936.

DAVIS, E. H. "We Found the Cave of Lost Art," *Desert Magazine* (Palm Desert), XII, No. 4 (1949), 25–27.

DEETZ, J. F. "A Dateable Chumash Pictograph from Santa Barbara County," *American Antiquity* (Salt Lake City, University of Utah Press), Vol. XXIX, No. 4 (1964).

DE HARPORT, D. L. "An Archaeological Survey of Canyon de Chelly: Preliminary Report of the Field Sessions of 1948," *El Palacio*, LVIII, No. 2 (1951), 35–48.

DELABARRE, E. B. *Dighton Rock—A Study of the Written Rocks of New England.* New York: Walter Neal, 1928.

DE LAGUNA, FREDERICA. "Peintures Rupestries Eskimo," *Journal de la Société des Américanistes* (Paris), n.s. Vol. XXV (1933).

——. *The Archaeology of Cook Inlet.* Philadelphia: University of Pennsylvania Press, 1934.

——. "Chugach Prehistory," *Publications in Anthropology* (Seattle, University of Washington Press), XIII (1956), 102–109.

DEWDNEY, SELWYN. "Stone Age Art in the Canadian Shield," *Canadian Art*, XVI (1959) 164–167.

——. *Indian Art.* Saskatchewan Museum of Natural History Popular Series No. 4. Regina, 1963.

——. "Writings on Stone Along the Milk River," *The Beaver* (Winnipeg), Winter 1964.

——. *Stone Age Paintings.* Department of Mines and Natural Resources, Manitoba, 1965.

——, and KIDD, KENNETH E. *Indian Rock Paintings of the Great Lakes.* Toronto: University of Toronto Press, 1962.

DIESING, E. H., and MAGRE, F. "Petroglyphs and Pictographs in Missouri," *The Missouri Archaeologist*, Vol. VIII, No. 1 (1942).

DIGUET, L. "Note sur la pictographie de la Basse-Californie," *Anthropologie* (Paris), 1894, pp. 160–175.

——. "Rapport sur une mission scientifique dans la Basse-Californie," *Nouvelle Archives des Missions Scientifiques* (Paris), IX (1899), 1–53.

DITTERT, A. E., JR., HESTER, J. J., and EDDY, F. W. *An Archaeological Survey of the Navajo Reservoir District, Northwestern New Mexico*. A monograph of the School of American Research and the Museum of New Mexico, No. 23. Santa Fe, 1961.

DURHAM, D. "Petroglyphs at Mesa de los Padillas," *El Palacio*, Vol. LXII, No. 1 (January 1955).

DUTTON, B. P. *Sun Father's Way—The Kiva Murals of Kuaua*. Albuquerque: University of New Mexico Press, 1963.

EBERHART, H., and BABCOCK, AGNES. *An Archaeological Survey of Mutau Flat, Ventura County, California*. Contributions to California Archaeology, No. 5. Los Angeles, 1963.

ELROD, M. J. *Pictured Rocks, Indian Writings on the Rock Cliffs of Flathead Lake, Montana*. Bulletin of the University of Montana, No. 46, Biological Series No. 14. Missoula, 1908.

ELSASSER, A. B., and CONTRERAS, E. "Modern Petrography in Central California and Western Nevada," Reports of the University of California Archaeological Survey (Berkeley), No. 41 (1958), pp. 12–18.

EMMONS, G. T. "Petroglyphs in Southeastern Alaska," *American Anthropologist*, X (1908), 221–230.

ENGERRAND, J. *Nuevos Petroglifos de la Baja California*. Boletin del Museo Nacional de Arqueologia, Historia e Etnologia, No. 10, Mexico City.

————. *Nota Complementaria acera de los Petrogliphos de la Baja California, ibid.*

ERWIN, R. P. "Indian Rock Writing in Idaho," 12th Annual Report, Idaho Historical Society, Boise, 1930, pp. 35–111.

EWERS, J. C. *Plains Indian Painting*. Stanford: Stanford University Press, 1939.

FENENGA, F. *Methods of Recording and Present Status of Knowledge Concerning Petroglyphs in California*. University of California Archaeological Survey, No. 3. Berkeley, 1949.

FERGUSSON, G. J., and LIBBY, W. F. *UCLA Radiocarbon Dates II*. Los Angeles, University of California Institute of Geophysics. 1962.

————. *UCLA Radiocarbon Dates III*. Los Angeles, University of California Institute of Geophysics. 1963.

FEWKES, J. W. "A Few Tusayan Pictographs," *American Anthropologist*, o.s. V, No. 1 (1892). 9–26.

————. "Tusayan Totemic Signatures," *ibid.*, No. 1 (1897), 1–11.

————. "Tusayan Migration Traditions," Nineteenth Annual Report of the Bureau of American Ethnology, Part 2. Washington, D.C., 1900.

————. "Hopi Katcinas," Twenty-first Annual Report of the Bureau of American Ethnology. Washington, D.C., 1903, pp. 3–126.

————. *Preliminary Report on a Visit to the Navaho National Monument, Arizona*. Bureau of American Ethnology Bulletin, No. 50. Washington, D.C., 1911.

FINLEY, R. S. "Note on the Orizaba Pictograph (Olson's) Cave, Santa Cruz Island, Santa Barbara, California," National Speleological Society, Monthly Report of the Stanford Grotto (Palo Alto, California), 1951.

FLAMAND, G. B. M. *Les Pierres écrites (Hadjrat-Mektoubat): Gravures et inscriptions rupestres du Nord-africain.* Paris: Massonet Cie., Editeurs, 1921.

FOLMANN, GERHARD. "Lichenometrische Altersbestimmungen an vorchristlichen Steinsetzungen der Polynesischen Osterinsel," *Naturwissenschaften* (Berlin), 1961, pp. 627–628.

FOSSNOCK, A. "Pictographs and Murals in the Southwest," *El Palacio*, XXXIX, Nos. 16–18 (1935), 81–90.

FOSTER, G. "Petrographic Art in Glen Canyon," *Plateau* (Flagstaff), XXVII, No. 1 (1954), 6–18.

FREDERICK, M. C. "Some Indian Paintings," *Land of Sunshine*, XV, No. 4 (1901), 223–227.

FUNDABURK, L. *Sun Circles and Human Hands.* (Privately printed; Luverne, Alabama, 1957.)

GALLENKAMP, C. "Where Ancients Wrote in Stone," *Desert Magazine* (Palm Desert), XVIII, No. 5 (1955), 16–18.

GALLOWAY, E., and AGOGINO, G. A. "Pictographs at Wall Rock Cave, Albany County, Wyoming," *The Wyoming Archaeologist* (Sheridan), Vol. V, No. 3 (September 1962).

GANONG, W. F. *Upon Aboriginal Pictographs Reported From New Brunswick.* Bulletin of the Natural History Society of New Brunswick, Vol. V, No. 22, Part II. Saint John, 1904.

GARDNER, ERLE STANLEY. "The Case of the Baja Caves," *Life*, LIII (1962), 62–64.

———, *The Hidden Heart of Baja.* New York: William Morrow & Company, 1962.

GEBHARD, DAVID. "Petroglyphs of Wyoming: A Preliminary Paper," *El Palacio*, LVIII, No. 3 (1951), 67–81.

———. "Petroglyphs in the Boysen Basin, Wyoming," University of Wyoming Publication, XVIII, No. 1 (1954), 66–70.

———. "Pictographs in the Sierra Blanca Mountains," *El Palacio*, LXIV, No. 3 (1957), 215–222.

———. "Hidden Lake Pictographs," *El Palacio*, LXVIII, No. 4 (1958), 146–149.

———. "Nineteen Centuries of American Abstraction," *Art News*, LIX, No. 10 (1958), 20–23.

———. *Prehistoric Paintings of the Diablo Region of Western Texas.* Roswell Museum Publications in Art and Science, No. 3. Roswell, New Mexico, 1960.

———. "Prehistoric Rock Drawings at Painted Grotto, New Mexico," *El Palacio*, Vol. LXIX, No. 4 (1962).

———. "Rock Drawings in the Western United States," *Jahrbuch fur Prahistorische und Ethnographische Kunst* (Berlin), Vol. XX, 1963.

———. "The Shield Motif in Plains Rock Art," *American Antiquity*, 1966.

———, AGOGINO, A., and HAYNES, V. "Horned Owl Cave, Wyoming," *ibid.*, XXIX, No. 3 (1964), 360–368.

———, and CAHN, H. A. "The Petroglyphs of Dinwoody, Wyoming," *ibid.*, XV, No. 3 (1950), 219–228.

GIDDINGS, J. L. "Rock Paintings in Central Alaska," *ibid.*, Vol. VII, No. 1 (1941).

GILBERT, H. "Indian Picture Writing," *The Wyoming Archaeologist*, Vol. V, No. 3 (September 1962).

GJESSING, GUTORM. "Petroglyphs and Pictographs in British Columbia," in *Indian Tribes of Aboriginal America*. Selected Papers of the Twenty-ninth International Congress of Americanists, 1952, pp. 66–79.

——. "Petroglyphs and Pictographs in the Coast Salishan Area of Canada," in *Miscellanea Paul Rivet*. Publicationes del Instituto de Historia, Primera Serie, No. 50. Mexico City, 1958. Pp. 257–275.

GLADWIN, H. G., *Men Out of Asia*. New York: McGraw-Hill Book Company, 1947.

——. *A History of the Ancient Southwest*. Portland, Maine: Bond Wheelwright, 1957.

——, HAURY, E. W., SAYLES, E. B., and GLADWIN, N., "Excavations at Snaketown—Material Culture." Medallion papers, No. XXV. (Privately printed; Gila Pueblo: Globe, Arizona.)

GODDARD, P. E. *Life and Culture of the Hupa*. University of California Publications in American Archaeology and Ethnology, Vol. I, No. 1. Berkeley, 1903.

GOODALL, E., COOKE, C. K., and CLARK, J. D. *Prehistoric Rock Art of Central Africa*. National Publications Trust, Salisbury, Southern Rhodesia, 1959.

GRANT, CAMPBELL. "Prehistoric Paintings of the Santa Barbara Region," Santa Barbara Museum of Natural History, Museum Talk, 1960.

——. "Ancient Art in the Wilderness," *Pacific Discovery* (San Francisco), July–August 1961.

——. "Cave Paintings of the Chumash." *Arts* (New York), May–June 1962.

——. "California's Painted Caves," *Desert Magazine* (Palm Desert), May 1964.

——. *A Collection of Chumash Artifacts from the Sierra Madre Mountains of Santa Barbara County, California*. University of California Archaeological Survey, No. 63. Berkeley, 1964.

——. "California's Legacy of Indian Rock Art," *Natural History Magazine* (New York), June 1964.

——. "Rock Painting in California," *Jahrbuch fur Prahistorische und Ethnographische Kunst*, Vol. XXI (1965).

——. *The Rock Paintings of the Chumash*. Berkeley: University of California Press, 1965.

——. *Prehistoric Rock Art of the Santa Barbara Region*. An illustrated catalogue of an exhibit of rock painting facsimiles at the Art Gallery, University of California at Santa Barbara, Oct. 12–Nov. 7, 1965.

——. "Cave Paintings of Sonora," *Desert Magazine* (Palm Desert), April 1967.

GRAZIOSI, P. *Palaeolithic Art*. New York: McGraw-Hill Book Company, 1960.

GREEN, E. "Ancient Rock Inscriptions in Johnson County, Arkansas," in *Miscellaneous Papers Relating to Anthropology*. Annual Report of the Smithsonian Institution (Washington, D.C.) 1881, pp. 538–541.

GREEN, W. "Cave Painting in Ventura County." Unpublished MS in author's collection, 1935.

GREER, E. S., JR. "More 'Mystery Holes in Rock,'" *Journal of Alabama Archaeology*, Vol. IX, No. 2 (1963).

GREY, D., and SWEEM, G. D. "Pictograph Classification and Petroglyph Weathering," *The Wyoming Archaeologist*, Vol. IV, No. 2 (1961).

GRIMSHAW, RUSS, and MAY, CLYDE. "Lucerne Valley Pictographs," *The Wyoming Archaeologist*, VI, No. 4 (December 1963), 8–12.

GRUBER, A. "A Survey of Petroglyphs in Black Canyon," *The Southwest Museum Masterkey* (Los Angeles), Vol. XXXV, No. 3 (July–September 1961).

HAINES, F. "How the Indian Got the Horse," *American Heritage* (New York), 1964.

HALLISEY, N., "Sketches of Rock Paintings up the Styne Valley Near Lytton, B. C.," *British Columbia Digest*, April 1964, (Quesnel).

HARNER, M. J. "Gravel Pictographs of the Lower Colorado River Region," Reports of the University of California Archaeological Survey, No. 22. Berkeley, 1953, pp. 1–32.

HAURY, E. W. *Painted Cave: Northeastern Arizona*. Amerind Foundation Inc., No. 3, 1945.

HEDDON, M. "Surface Printing as a Method of Recording Petroglyphs," *American Antiquity*, XXIII (1958), 435–439.

HEIZER, ROBERT F. *Petroglyphs from Southwestern Kodiak Islands, Alaska*. Proceedings of the American Philosophical Society. Philadelphia, 1947, pp. 284–293.

———. *Sacred Rain Rocks of Northern California*. University of California Archaeological Survey, No. 20. Berkeley, 1953.

———., and BAUMHOFF, MARTIN A. *Prehistoric Rock Art of Nevada and Eastern California*. Berkeley: University of California Press, 1962.

HENDERSON, R. "Glyph Hunters in the Indian Country," *Desert Magazine* (El Centro), X, No. 1 (1946), 11–15.

HESTER, J. J. *Early Navajo Migrations and Acculturation in the Southwest*. Museum of New Mexico Papers in Anthropology, No. 6. Santa Fe, 1962.

HIBBEN, F. C. *A Possible Pyramidal Structure and Other Mexican Influences at Pottery Mound, New Mexico*. American Antiquity, Vol. 31, No. 4 (1966), 522–529.

HINTHORN, J. "Turner Ranch Pictographs," *The Wyoming Archaeologist*, Vol. V, No. 4 (December 1962).

HODGE, F. W. *Handbook of the American Indians North of Mexico*. Bureau of American Ethnology Bulletin, No. 30. Washington, D.C., 1907.

HUNT, C. B. "Desert Varnish," *Science*, CXX, No. 3109 (1954), 183–184.

HURST, C. T., and HENDRICKS, L. J. "Some Unusual Petroglyphs near Sapinero, Colorado," *Southwestern Lore* (Gunnison), XVIII, No. 1 (1952), 14–18.

HURT, W. L., JR. "A Method for Cataloguing Pictographs," *New Mexico Anthropologist* (Albuquerque), III, Nos. 3–4 (1939), 40–44.

HUSCHER, B. H., and HUSCHER, H. A. "Conventionalized Bear-Track Petroglyphs of the Uncompahgre Plateau," *Southwestern Lore*, VI, No. 2 (1940), 25–28.

INVERARITY, R. B. *Art of the Northwest Coast Indians*. Berkeley: University of California Press, 1950.

IOVIN, JUNE. "A Summary of Luiseño Material Culture," University of California Archaeological Survey Annual Report, 1962–1963, Los Angeles, pp. 79–134.

IRVING, WILLIAM N. "Field Work in the Western Brooks Range, Alaska: Preliminary Report," *Arctic Anthropology*, Vol. I, No. 1 (1961).

IRWIN, MARGARET C. "Petroglyphs Near Santa Barbara," Santa Barbara Museum of Natural History, Museum Talk, 1950, pp. 1–5.

JACKSON, A. T. *Picture-Writing of Texas Indians*. Bureau of Research in the Social Sciences, Study No. 27. Austin: University of Texas Press, 1938.

JASMANN, ALICE O. *Archaeology in Montana*. Montana Archaeological Society (Helena), Vol. III. No. 3. January 1962.

JENNESS, DIAMOND. *Archaeological Investigations in Bering Strait*. National Museum of Canada Bulletin, No. 50. Ottawa.

KEITHAHN, EDWARD L. "The Petroglyphs of Southeastern Alaska," *American Antiquity*, Vol. VI, No. 2 (1940), 123–132.

KELLEY, C. "Murals Painted by Ancient Tribesmen," *Desert Magazine* (Palm Desert), XIII, No. 8 (1950), 11–12.

KELLEY, J. C. "Atlatls, Bows and Arrows, Pictographs, and the Pecos River Focus," *American Antiquity*, XVI, No. 1 (1950), 71–74.

KETTL, J. W. "Project Petroglyphs," *Southwest Museum Masterkey*, Vol. XXXVI (January–March 1962).

KIDDER, A. V., and GUERNSEY, S. J. *Archaeological Explorations in Northwestern Arizona*. Bureau of American Ethnology Bulletin, No. 65. Washington, D.C., 1919.

KING, D. R., and DEWDNEY, SELWYN. "Prehistoric Rock Art in Alberta." To be published by Glenbow Foundation of Archaeology.

KIRKLAND, F. *A Description of Texas Pictographs*. Bulletin of Texas Archaeological and Paleontological Society (Abilene), X (1938), 11–39.

KLEIBER, H., and LEWIS, O. "Dinwoody Lakes Pictograph Site," *The Wyoming Archaeologist*, Vol. V, No. 4 (December 1962).

KROEBER, A. L. *Handbook of the Indians of California*. Bureau of American Ethnology Bulletin, No. 78. Washington D.C., 1925.

KUHN, H. *Wenn Steine Reden*. Wiesbaden: Brockhaus, 1966.

LA MONK, CHARLES S. "Pictograph Cave, Burro Flats," Archaeological Survey Association of Southern California *Newsletter* (Los Angeles), I, No. 2 (1953), 8–9.

———. "Painted Rock," *ibid.*, Vol. II, No. 4 (1954), 3–5.

LA PAZ, L. "Meteoritical Pictographs," Contributions of the Meteoritical Society, IV, No. 2, 122–128. Los Angeles, 1948.

LATHRAP, D. *A Distinctive Pictograph from the Carrizo Plains, San Luis Obispo County*. University of California Archaeological Survey, No. 9, 1950.

LATTA, F. F. *Handbook of the Yokuts Indians*. Oildale, California: Bear State Books, 1949.

LAUDERMILK, J. D. "On the Origin of Desert Varnish," *American Journal of Science* (New Haven), Fifth Series, XXI, No. 121 (1931), 51–66.

LAWSON, A. C. "Ancient Rock Inscriptions on the Lake of the Woods," *American Naturalist*, XIX (1885), 654–657.

LAWTON, SHERMAN P. "Petroglyphs and Pictographs in Oklahoma: An Introduction," *Plains Anthropologist*, Vol. VII, No. 17 (1962).

LEECHMAN, DOUGLAS, HESS, MARGARET, and FOWLER, ROY L. *Pictographs in Southwestern Alberta*. Bulletin No. 136, Annual Report of the National Museum. Ottawa, 1953–54.

——, et al. *Some Pictographs of Southeastern British Columbia*. Transactions of the Royal Society of Canada, Third Series, XLVIII (1954), 77–85.

LEONARD, ZENAS. *Narrative of the Adventures of Zenas Leonard*. Norman: University of Oklahoma Press, 1959.

LEWIS, T. H. "Incised Boulders in the Upper Mississippi Valley," *American Naturalist*, September 1889.

LEWIS, T. M. N., and KNEBERG, M., eds. *Ten Years of the Tennessee Archaeologist: Selected Subjects*. Knoxville: University of Tennessee, 1954.

LHOTE, H. *The Search for the Tassili Frescoes*. New York: E. P. Dutton & Co., 1959.

LIBBY, WILLARD F. *Radiocarbon Dating*. Chicago: The University of Chicago Press, 1955.

MAC GOWAN, KENNETH. *Early Man in the New World*. New York: The Macmillan Company, 1950.

MAC NEISH, RICHARD S. "Preliminary Investigations in the Sierra de Tamaulipas, Mexico," American Philosophical Society, Vol. 48, Part 6, 1958.

——. "The Origins of New World Civilization," *Scientific American*, Vol. CCXI, No. 5 (1964).

MC ADAMS, W. *Records of Ancient Races in the Mississippi Valley*. St. Louis: Barns, 1887.

MC KUSICK, M. *Men of Ancient Iowa*. Ames: Iowa State University Press, 1964.

MAGRE, FRANK. "The Petrographs of Missouri." Unpublished MS in the possession of the author.

MALLERY, GARRICK. *Pictographs of the North American Indians*. Fourth Annual Report of the Bureau of American Ethnology. Washington, D.C., 1886.

——. *Picture Writing of the American Indians*. Tenth Annual Report of the Bureau of American Ethnology. Washington, D.C., 1893.

MALOUF, CARLING. *Pictographs and Petroglyphs*. Archaeological Society of Montana, Vol. III, No. 1 (1961).

MASON, J. ALDEN. *Some Unusual Petroglyphs and Pictographs of Durango and Coahuila, Mexico*. Homenaje a Pablo Martinez del Rio, Instituto Nacional de Antropologia e Historia. Mexico, 1961.

MAYNARD, C. C. "Hieroglyphics Near Benjamin, Utah," *Improvement Era* (Salt Lake City), 1911, pp. 582–591.

MEIGHAN, CLEMENT W. "Prehistoric Rock Paintings in Baja California," *American Antiquity*, XXXI, No. 3 (January 1966), 372–392.

MILLER, W. C. "Two Possible Astronomical Pictographs Found in Northern Arizona," *Plateau*, XXVII, No. 4 (1955), 6–13.

MITCHELL, J. R. "Petroglyphs and Pictographs in the Tennessee Valley and Surrounding Area: Part II," *Journal of Alabama Archaeology*, Vol. IX, No. 2 (1963).

MOMYER, G. *Indian Picture Writing in Southern California.* (Privately printed; San Bernardino, 1937).

MONTGOMERY, C. M. "The Corn Shrines of the Tanos," *Desert Magazine* (Palm Desert), Vol. XXVII, No. 12 (December 1964).

MORRISON, A. L. "The Painted Rocks of the Carisa (Carrizo Plains)," *National Motorist,* January 30, 1926.

MORSS, N. *The Ancient Culture of the Fremont River in Utah.* Papers of the Peabody Museum, Vol. XII, No. 3. Cambridge: Harvard University Press, 1931.

MOUNTFORD, C. P. "Art, Myth, and Symbolism," in *Records of the American-Australian Scientific Expedition to Arnhem Land.* Vol. I. Melbourne, 1956.

MULLOY, W. *A Preliminary Historical Outline for the Northwest Plains.* University of Wyoming Publications, Vol. XXII, No. 1. Laramie, 1958.

NEWCOMBE, C. F. "Petroglyphs in British Columbia," *Victoria Daily Times,* September 7, 1907.

NIBLACK, A. P. "The Coast Indians of Southern Alaska and Northern British Columbia," Annual Report for 1887–88, U.S. National Museum. Washington, D.C., 1890, pp. 225–386.

OBERMAIER, H., and WEINERT, P. *Las Pinturas Rupestres del Narranco de Valltorta.* Madrid: Castellon, 1919.

ORELLANA, R. *Petroglifos y Pinturas Rupestres de Sonora.* Organo oficial del Centro de Investigaciones antropologicas de Mexico, Vol. I. Mexico City, 1953.

ORR, PHIL C. "Who Painted Painted Cave?" Archaeological Survey Association of Southern California *Newsletter,* II, No. 2 (1954), 7–8.

OSBURN, D. N. "Petroglyph and Pictograph Sites in the Finlay Mountains," *Field and Laboratory* (Southern Methodist University), IX, No. 1 (1941), 30–35.

OVER, W. H. *Indian Picture Writing in South Dakota.* University of South Dakota Archaeological Circular, No. 4, 1941.

PARKER, M. "A Study of the Rocky Creek Pictoglyph," *Tennessee Archaeologist* (Knoxville), Vol. V, No. 2 (1948).

PAYEN, L. A. "Petroglyphs of Sacramento and Adjoining Counties," University of California Archaeological Survey. Berkeley, 1959.

PEITHMAN, IRVING M. "Pictographs and Petroglyphs in Southern Illinois," *Journal of Illinois State Archaeological Society* (Springfield), Vol. II, No. 4 (1952).

———. "A Petroglyph Site at Fountain Bluff, Jackson County, Illinois," *Central States Archaeological Journal* (Carbondale), II, No. 1 (1955), pp. 11–13.

PEPPER, CHORAL. "Bewitched by Baja," *Desert Magazine* (Palm Desert), Vol. XXVII, No. 8 (August 1964).

———. "Petroglyphs, the Unsolved Mystery," *ibid.,* Vol. XXVI, No. 11 (November 1964).

PERRYMAN, M. "Georgia Petroglyphs," *Archaeology* (New York), 1964, pp. 54–56.

PETERSEN, EUGENE T. "Michigan's Mysterious Rock Painting," *Ford Times,* July 1960.

POMPA Y POMPA, ANTONIO. "La Escritura Petroglifica Rupestre y su Expresion en el Noroeste Mexicano," *Anales* (Mexico, Instituto Nacional de Antropologia e Historia), Epoca 6a, 1956, pp. 213–225.

PRENTICE, R. A. "Pictograph Story of Konate," *El Palacio*, LVIII, No. 3 (1951), 90–96.

Present Status of Knowledge Concerning Petroglyphs in Nova Scotia. Nova Scotia Museum. Halifax, 1956.

RAFN, C. C. *Antiquites Americanae*. Plate 13. Copenhagen, 1845.

REAGAN, A. B. "The Pictographs of Ashley and Dry Fork Valleys in Northeastern Utah," *Transactions* of the Kansas Academy of Science (Topeka), XXXIV (1931), 168–216.

———. "Some Notes on the Picture Writing North of Mexico," Bulletin of the Wagner Free Institute of Science of Philadelphia, VII, No. 4 (1932), 38–54.

———. *Some Notes on an Ancient Culture of the Provo-Salt Lake Region*. Reprinted from *Northwest Science*, Vol. IX, No. 2 (1935).

RENAUD, E. B. *Archaeological Survey of Eastern Colorado, First Report*. University of Denver, Department of Anthropology, 1931.

———. *Archaeological Survey of Eastern Wyoming, Summer 1931*. University of Denver, Department of Anthropology, and University of Wyoming. Denver, 1932.

———. *Archaeological Survey of Eastern Colorado, Second Report*. University of Denver, Department of Anthropology, 1932.

———. *Archaeological Survey of Eastern Colorado, Third Report*. University of Denver, Department of Anthropology, 1933.

———. *Archaeological Survey of the High Western Plains, Eighth Report*. University of Denver, Department of Anthropology, 1936.

———. *Archaeological Survey of North Central New Mexico, Eleventh Report*. University of Denver, Department of Anthropology, 1938.

———. *Archaeology of the High Western Plains, Seventeen Years of Archaeological Research*. University of Denver, Department of Anthropology, 1947.

RICHARDS, A., and RICHARDS, D. "Petroglyphs of the Russell Site," in *Science of Man, I*, No. 1 (1960), 18–21.

RICHARDS, D. J. *The Sanilac Petroglyphs*. Cranbrook Institute of Science, Bulletin 36. Bloomfield Hills, Michigan, 1958.

RITTER, D. "Petroglyphs, a Few Outstanding Sites," Oregon Archaeological Society *Screenings* (Portland), Vol. XIV, No. 8 (1965).

RITZENTHALER, R. E. "Wisconsin Petroglyphs and Pictographs," *Wisconsin Archaeologist*, XXXI, No. 4 (1950), 83–129.

ROSS, E. T. "A Preliminary Survey of the Petroglyphs of Southern California." Unpublished MS, 1938.

ROZAIRE, C. E. "Pictographs at Burro Flats," Ventura Historical Society Quarterly, February 1959.

———, and KRITZMAN, C. "A Petroglyph Cave on San Nicolas Island," *Southwest Museum Masterkey*, Vol. XXXIV, No. 4 (1960).

RUDY, J. R. *Archaeological Survey of Western Utah*. University of Utah Anthropological Paper No. 12. Salt Lake City, 1953.

RUL, FRANCISCO GONZALEZ. *Petroglifos en un Lugar Denominado "El Sol."* Homenaje a Pablo Martinez del Rio, Instituto Nacional de Antropologia e Historia. Mexico, 1961.

SCHAAFSMA, POLLY. "Rock Art of the Navajo Reservoir," *El Palacio*, Vol. LXIX, No. 4 (1962).

———. *Rock Art in the Navajo Reservoir District.* Museum of New Mexico Papers in Anthropology, No. 7. Santa Fe: Museum of New Mexico Press, 1963.

———. *Southwest Indian Pictographs and Petroglyphs.* Santa Fe: Museum of New Mexico Press, 1965.

———. *Early Navajo Rock Paintings and Carvings.* Museum of Navaho Ceremonial Art, Sante Fe, 1966.

SCHOOLCRAFT, H. R. *Historical and Statistical Information Respecting the Indians of the United States.* Vol. II: plate 41; Vol. III: plate 41. Philadelphia: J. B. Lippincott Company, 1852–54.

SECRIST, K. G. *Pictographs in Central Montana.* Part I: *Fergus County.* Montana State University Anthropology and Sociology Papers, No. 20. Missoula, 1960.

SETZLER, F. M. "Seeking the Secret of the Giants," *National Geographic Magazine*, Vol. CII, No. 3 (1952).

SHUMATE, MAYNARD. *Pictographs in Central Montana.* Part II: *Panels Near Great Falls, Montana.* Montana State University Anthropology and Sociology Papers, No. 21. Missoula, 1960.

SHUTLER, R., and SHUTLER, M. E. *Archaeological Survey in Southern Nevada.* Nevada State Museum Anthropological Papers, No. 7. Reno, 1962.

SIMS, A. C. "An Artist Analyses New Mexico's Petroglyphs," *El Palacio*, LV, No. 10 (1948), 302–309.

———. *San Cristobal Petroglyphs.* Santa Fe: Southwest Editions, 1950.

SKINNER, A. *A Staten Island Petroglyph.* Heye Foundation Indian Notes, Vol. X. New York, 1925.

SMITH, G. A., *et al. Indian Picture Writing of San Bernardino and Riverside Counties.* San Bernardino County Museum Association Publication, Vol. 7, No. 3, 1961.

SMITH, H. I. *An Album of Prehistoric Canadian Art.* Victoria Memorial Museum, Bulletin 37. Ottawa, 1923.

———. "A List of Petroglyphs in British Columbia," *American Anthropologist*, XXIX, No. 4 (1927), 605–610.

———. "A Pictograph on the Lower Skeena River, British Columbia," *ibid.*, pp. 611–614.

SMITH, M. W. "Petroglyph Complexes in the History of the Columbia-Fraser Region," *Southwestern Journal of Anthropology* (Santa Fe), II, No. 3 (1946), 306–322.

SMITH, V. "Sheep Hunting Artists of Black Canyon Walls," *Desert Magazine*, VII, No. 5 (1944), 5–7.

SMITH, W. *Kiva Mural Decorations at Awatovi and Kawaika-a, with a Survey of Other Wall Paintings in the Pueblo Southwest.* Papers of the Peabody Museum, Vol. 37, No. 5. Cambridge: Harvard University Press, 1952.

SNOW, DEAN R. "Petroglyphs of Southern Minnesota," *The Minnesota Archaeologist*, XXIV, No. 4 (October 1962), 102–128.

SOLECKI, RALPH S. "A Petrograph in Northern Alaska," *American Antiquity*, XVIII, No. 1 (1952), 63–64.

SOLLAS, W. J. *Ancient Hunters*. New York: The Macmillan Company, 1924.

STEWARD, JULIAN H. *Petroglyphs of California and Adjoining States*. University of California Publications in American Archaeology and Ethnology, Vol. 24, No. 2. Berkeley, 1929.

———. "Petroglyphs of the United States," Annual Report of the Smithsonian Institution. Washington, D.C., 1936.

———. *Archaeological Reconnaissance of Southern Utah*. Smithsonian Institution Bulletin, No. 128. Washington, D.C., 1941.

STRONG, E. *Stone Age on the Columbia River*. Portland, Oregon: Binfords and Mort, 1959.

STRONG, W. D., and SCHENCK, W. E. "Petroglyphs near The Dalles of the Columbia River," *American Anthropology*, XXVII, (1925), 77–90.

———, ———, and STEWARD, J. H. *Archaeology of The Dalles-Deschutes Region*. University of California Publications in American Archaeology and Ethnology, Vol. 29, No. 1. Berkeley and Los Angeles, 1930.

SWANTON, J. D. *The Indian Tribes of North America*. Bureau of American Ethnology Bulletin, No. 145. Washington, D.C., 1953.

SWAUGER, JAMES L. "An X-Ray Figure on the Timmons Farm Petroglyphs Site, 46-Oh-64," *The West Virginia Archaeologist* (Moundsville), No. 14, February 1962.

———. "Petroglyphs at the Hamilton Farm Site, Monongalia County, West Virginia," *ibid.*, No. 15, February 1963.

———. "The Table Rock Petroglyphs Site, 46-Oh-38," *ibid.*, No. 16, December 1963.

———. *The East Liverpool Petroglyph Data: A Tribute*. Reprint from *Pennsylvania Archaeologist* (Philadelphia, Bulletin of the Society for Pennsylvania Archaeology), Vol. XXXIII, No. 3 (1963).

———. "The Francis Farm Petroglyphs Site, 36-Fa-35," *ibid.*, Vol. XXXIV, No. 2 (1964).

———. "The New Geneva Petroglyphs Site, 36-Fa-37," *ibid.*

SWEETMAN, P. W. "A Preliminary Report on the Peterborough Petroglyphs," *Ontario History*, Vol. XLVII, No. 3 (1955).

SWIFT, R. H. "Prehistoric Paintings in Santa Barbara," Southern California Archaeological Society Publication, No. 3, 1931, pp. 35–38.

TAFT, G. E. "An Arizona Pictograph," *American Antiquarian* (Philadelphia), XXXV (1913), 140–145.

TANNER, C. L., and CONNOLLY, F. "Petroglyphs of the Southwest," Kiva (Tucson), III, No. 4 (1938), 13–16.

TATUM, R. M. "Distribution and Bibliography of the Petroglyphs of the United States," *American Antiquity*, XII, No. 2 (1946), 122–125.

———. "The Importance of Petroglyphs in Tennessee," *Tennessee Archaeologist*, III, No. 2 (1946), 40–41.

TAYLOR, H. C. *An Archaeological Reconnaissance in Northern Coahuila*. Bulletin of the Texas Archaeological and Paleontological Society, Vol. 19. Lubbock, 1848. Pp. 74–87.

TEIT, JAMES A. *A Rock Painting of the Thompson River Indians, British Columbia*. American Museum of Natural History Bulletin, 1896. Pp. 227–230.

————. "The Salishan Tribes of the Western Plateaus," in Franz Boas, ed., Forty-fifth Annual Report of the Bureau of American Ethnology, 1930, pp. 23–396.

TREGANZA, A. E. "An Archaeological Reconnaissance of Northeastern Baja California and Southeastern California," *American Antiquity*, VIII, No. 2 (1942), 160–161.

TRUE, D. L. "Pictographs of the San Luis Rey Basin," *ibid.*, XX, No. 1 (1954), 68–72.

TRUMBO, T. M. "Ancient Artist Lived on Rattlesnake Peak," *Desert Magazine* (Palm Desert), XII, No. 8 (1949), 13–16.

TURNER, CHRISTY G. *Petrographs of the Glen Canyon Region*. Museum of Northern Arizona, Bulletin 38, Glen Canyon Series, No. 4. Flagstaff, 1963.

UNDERHILL, R. M. *Red Man's America*. Chicago: University of Chicago Press, 1953.

VAN VALKENBURGH, R. "We Found the Glyphs in the Guijus," *Desert Magazine* (El Centro), IX, No. 3 (1946), 17–20.

VOEGLIN, E. W. *Tubatulabal Ethnography*. University of California Anthropological Records, Vol. 2, No. 1. Berkeley, 1938.

VON WERLHOF, J. C. "Granite Galleries," *Pacific Discovery*, Vol. XI, No. 4 (July–August 1958).

————. *Rock Art of the Owens Valley, California*. University of California Archaeological Survey, No. 65. Berkeley, 1965.

WATERS, F. *Book of the Hopi*. New York: Viking Press, 1963.

WETHERILL, M. A. "Pictographs at Betatakin Ruin," U.S. National Park Service Southwestern Monuments Monthly Report. Santa Fe, May 1935, pp. 263–264.

WILBURN, H. C. *Judaculla Rock*. Southern Indian Studies, Vol. IV, October 1952.

WILLOUGHBY, C. C. *Antiquities of the New England Indians*. Papers of the Peabody Museum. Cambridge: Harvard University Press, 1935.

WINTEMBERG, W. J. *Petroglyphs of Roche Percee and Vicinity, Saskatchewan*. Transactions of the Royal Society of Canada, Third Series, XXXIII (1939), 175–184.

WITTY, THOMAS A., JR. *Archaeological Investigations of the Hell Creek Valley in the Wilson Reservoir, Russell and Lincoln Counties, Kansas*. Kansas State Historical Society Anthropological Series 1, 1962.

WOODS, E. B. *La Piedra Pintada de la Carrisa*. (Privately printed, 1900.)

WORMINGTON, H. M. *A Reappraisal of the Fremont Culture*. Denver Museum of Natural History Proceedings, No. 1, 1955.

————, and LISTER, R. H. *Archaeological Investigations on the Uncompahgre Plateau in West Central Colorado*. Denver Museum of Natural History Proceedings, No. 2, 1956.

YATES, L. G. "Indian Pictoglyphs in California," *Overland Monthly*, 2d Series, 1896, pp. 657–661.

YOUNG, J. V. "The Peregrinations of Kokopelli," *Westways* (Los Angeles), Vol. LVII, No. 9 (1965).

INDEX